Fund-raising

Fund-raising

A comprehensive handbook

Hilary Blume

Routledge & Kegan Paul

London, Henley and Boston

First published in 1977
by Routledge & Kegan Paul Ltd
39 Store Street,
London WC1E 7DD,
Broadway House,
Newtown Road,
Henley-on-Thames,
Oxon RG9 1EN and
9 Park Street,
Boston, Mass. 02108, USA
Set in Baskerville
and printed in Great Britain by
Ebenezer Baylis & Son Ltd
The Trinity Press, Worcester, and London

ISBN 0 7100 8549 4

For my parents
Henry and Muriel Braverman

Contents

Acknowledgments

I should like to acknowledge the help of Janet Brannigan, my friend and colleague of many years; John Kingsbury, who taught me that fund-raising could be fun; Wendy Braverman for her advice on printing and advertising; Jacquie Salem for her helpful comments on publicity; Peter Gibson for his encouragement, and the benefit of his experience on groups; Jacques Depatie for his information on Oxfam (Québec) and Jean Desbiens for his information on the Federated Appeal of Montreal; and Mr Reed and Mr Ware of the Office of the Charity Commissioners for their helpful comments on that institution. For their information on trading activities, I should like to thank Peter Pascoe (National Society for the Mentally Handicapped Child), Roy Scott (Oxfam Trading) and Mr W. Painter (Barnardo's Publications Ltd). For information on appeals in broadcasting, I wish to thank the respective staffs of the BBC and ITA.

All in all, many people have been generous with their time and knowledge; my thanks to them all.

Introduction

This book is intended to help the many people who find themselves having to raise funds for charity. It seeks to suggest which methods might be appropriate both to the cause and the people trying to raise the money, and show how to go about organizing different types of appeals. Many people have some experience and understanding of some of the fund-raising techniques the book covers, yet may not have considered other methods. This book tries to give the benefits of experience, so that people can avoid learning through their mistakes and learn from other people's.

One point is emphasized throughout the book, and adherence to it will ensure avoidance of the most dismal fund-raising failures: never use the charity's resources as risk capital. Make sure that if no tickets are sold, or donations secured, the charity cannot lose much money. In other words, never organize an event with huge overheads that might not be recovered. Fund-raising usually involves some expense, for example, for postage and printing; but always make sure these are kept to a realistic level.

Some of the fund-raising methods described in this book may be used by organizations other than charities, for example, a local tennis club or a voluntary organization which campaigns for a change of legislation; but some methods, such as donations under covenant or from trusts, are open only to charities. Thus perhaps the first question to ask is, 'What is a charity, how to register, and what are the advantages of charitable status?'

Registering as a charity

There is often confusion as to quite what a charity is, and what benefits derive from charitable status. Voluntary, non-profit-making organizations are not necessarily charities. It is easy to register a charity as long as its aims fall within one or more of four categories:

1. The relief of poverty;
2. The furtherance of religion;
3. The advancement of education;
4. Other purposes of benefit to the community.

It is only the fourth category for which the charity has to show that it benefits a significant sector of the community; in other words, one could register as a charity an organization which advanced the education of a handful of people, but a recreation centre would have to cater for a wide section of the community for it to be considered charitable. Registration is very straightforward—it simply involves filling in a standard form. (All charities, except a few specifically excluded categories, are required by law to be registered.) Before registration, each charity has to have a trust deed, setting out its aims. A lawyer is usually needed to draw up the deed. Those wanting to set up a charity are well advised to contact the Charity Commissioners before drawing up the trust deed. The Charity Commissioners cannot draw up the actual deed, but will point out the pitfalls to be avoided. The trust deed sets out the purpose for which the charity is established, and is binding on its trustees. Once a charity is registered, neither the trustees, nor its founders, can by themselves alter the trust unless the trust deed specifically permits; and if the purpose of the charity has become outdated, then the Charity Commissioners have to be asked for an order of *cy près*, which changes the trust deed.

An anomaly has arisen from the requirement of the 1960 Charities Act that charities be registered, in that an assurance was given that those charities which were already established, yet whose aims might not be strictly charitable, would be registered. Some organizations now applying for registration may be rejected, as their objects are not regarded by the Charity Commissioners as charitable, whereas organizations with similar objectives may be registered, because they existed before 1960.

From time to time, *exposés* in the press point to some scandal in the charity world, and end in criticism of the Charity Commissioners for failing to deal with the situation. In fact, the Charity Commissioners are not government watchdogs, ensuring the efficient administration of charities. They can investigate complaints (which they say are few, and usually the result of misunderstandings) and remove trustees who are not fulfilling the trust deed. A charity, once registered, cannot cease to be a charity; if its objects are outdated its purpose can be changed by order of *cy près*; if grossly mismanaged, new trustees may be appointed by the Charity Commissioners; but it is still a charity.

There are definite advantages in being a registered charity, not least of which is the respectability which the public mistakenly believes it confers on organizations. The public regards registration as an endorsement of the worth of the organization, both in regard to its aims and its management. It is a view which is wholly misfounded, but which many charities exploit.

More tangible benefits of charitable status derive from tax concessions. A charity is exempt from income and corporation tax, from capital gains tax and, in most circumstances, from estate duty (or capital transfer tax). In addition, a registered charity enjoys a reduction of rates on its premises of 50 per cent, and more at the discretion of the local authority. Concessions are made to charities on land development tax. A myriad of statutes specifically exclude charities from obligations which they might find onerous. It is estimated that tax concessions on income and corporation tax (which the charity can reclaim under the covenant scheme) bring charities £20 million, and tax concessions to charities overall cost the taxpayer about £100 million a year.

What a fund-raiser can and cannot do for a charity

A fund-raiser must exploit the charity's assets to raise funds for its work. He must first assess the charity's funding needs. It is no use seeking £10,000 when the charity will founder if it does not have an income of £100,000. In some cases, it is appropriate to have a one-off appeal; in others, fund-raising has to be ongoing. For example, an appeal for a school building fund has a clearly defined aim; once the target amount has been reached the fund-raising can stop. It irritates donors who have been asked to give on a once-and-for-all basis to be re-approached, because the initial target figure was unrealistically low. Careful costing of the charity's needs must be done, with allowance for inflation, and some reserve against unforeseen contingencies. In some cases it is sensible to take professional advice in fixing the charity's financial needs, for example on building repair projects.

The fund-raiser must try to ensure that the target is realistic, and advise accordingly. For example, one therapeutic community for thirty disturbed adolescents drew up a shopping list of its needs which totalled over £200,000; it included furnishings of a luxurious quality. The fund-raiser had to point out that it was unlikely that any intelligent donor would respond to such an appeal—and if they did they would be alienated, once they saw how frivolously their money was spent. In other cases the target is fixed too low and it is up to the fund-raiser to pinpoint the need for a more ambitious appeal. It is not the fund-raiser's job to determine the policy of the charity, and tailor its needs to fit in with the appeal; but nor is it the fund-raiser's job to assume the burden of raising money for unrealistic campaigns.

Once the financial needs of the charity have been fixed, the fund-raiser should then consider from which sources the money may most easily be raised, and what assets the charity has which may be exploited. For example, has the charity any rich trustees who could raise the money from their friends and business colleagues? Is the cause likely to attract popular support, or is it likely to appeal to a small, specific group of people? (In the jargon of charity fund-raising this is known as constituency fund-raising.) If the charity is unknown but the cause is likely to have mass appeal, are there sufficient capital reserves to undertake a sustained advertising campaign? Is the cause likely to appeal to school children and, perhaps more important, to their teachers? Are women's groups likely to be sympathetic? It is important to pinpoint the precise group to which the charity will appeal, both by its cause and its style of achieving that cause. A good fund-raiser will be able to sense the tone of an organization, and assess what its assets are, and to whom it may most successfully go for funds.

Frequently people try to emulate the fund-raising successes of other charities, without considering whether these methods are appropriate to their own cause or not. Just because one charity raises £10,000 at a pop concert that does not mean all charities can raise £10,000 at pop concerts, even with the same group at the same venue; because one charity raises £200,000 at a dinner of twelve businessmen that does not mean all charities can raise £200,000 at such a dinner. Not all charities have equal appeal. Not all have influential trustees; and even good fund-raisers are not likely to be equally good at all aspects of fund-raising. It is important for the charity's trustees to choose the right type of fund-raiser, who is good at the kind of fund-raising appropriate to that charity. Usually it is easier to do this than to assess whether the person is competent.

Fund-raising is 50 per cent luck

All the skill, all the planning and all the competence of a fund-raiser cannot secure funds: to a great extent he must be lucky. With care, the fund-raiser can time an appeal so as to maximize the chance of success: he can assess the most likely sources of funds; he can, through skill, devise eye-catching literature—but he cannot create an economic boom, nor can he alter the weather. All fund-raising brings disappointments, and the fund-raiser must be temperamentally able to withstand them.

The most awful flops can be avoided if the fund-raiser thinks carefully beforehand and ensures that, if the worst comes to the worst, no money will be lost—simply none will be made. Specially organized events are particularly prone to disaster, and it is as well if a list of all the things that could go wrong is made at the planning stage. For example, if no tickets are sold; if it rains on an outdoor event; if no prior publicity is secured. If one has considered the possibility of something going wrong ahead of time, then one can consider possible remedies and avoid last-minute panic (which helps no one and infuriates volunteers).

Because all fund-raising involves some element of chance and the fund-raiser is constantly trying to reduce this element, it is unwise to plan campaigns too far in advance. The most effective campaigns are those undertaken in a very short time, in reaction to existing circumstances. This is not to say that prior planning cannot be done, but that it should be done in outline only, and the planners should retain flexibility. If, for example, an appeal is planned for a university library, and a few students throw a pot of red paint at a visiting lecturer, then the appeal may have to be re-timed, to allow time for the adverse publicity to subside. If the organizers of the appeal are not flexible, they will be unduly bothered by the need for delay, and probably when the appeal is launched it will be a rather limp, apologetic affair. Too often in charity fund-raising the planning is done too far in advance of time and the clerical work is left to the last minute. If planning a campaign which includes mailings, then the envelopes can be addressed (possibly by volunteers) well in advance; the contents of the envelopes can be printed nearer to the time of its launching.

Donor records

It is sensible to keep a record of past donations. The complexity of the donor file system depends on the numbers involved. For most charities a simple card file containing the name and address of the donor, the date and amount of the donation and, if known, the reason for the donation (e.g. annual appeal, Christmas cards) will be sufficient. The cards can be indexed under categories, for example, trusts, industry, groups, schools, individuals; or arranged geographically. (The Post Office offers a concession on large mailings which are pre-sorted in geographical areas.)

The donor file has many uses. A past donation signifies a sympathy with the cause which may, hopefully, yield further donations. If starting a local group, then the donor file can be used to find the names of possible supporters. Past donors can form the backbone of a charity's trading operation, of which some at least are likely to buy tickets or goods. Some fund-raisers expect to milk their past donors unremittingly, and can think of no fund-raising idea beyond yet another mailing to past donors. Nothing is more likely to alienate support than what comes to seem like harassment.

Donors may like to be kept informed of the charity's activities, and how their donation has helped the cause; usually an annual report which solicits further help is sufficient. If the charity has a newspaper, or quarterly information bulletin, then this can be sent to donors, but it will seem less wasteful if they are asked if they want to continue to receive it, say, after a year. People are always critical of money-wasting by charities, and will regard over-frequent appeals in this light.

A donor file is important in keeping a charity informed, so that in future appeals can be personalized. For example, if a trust has given before, but not a sufficiently large amount to warrant the preparation of a special appeal, a covering note can be added to the printed application, thanking the trustees for their past support and hoping it will continue. People who give to charity, even though they may be one amongst 10,000 donors, have an irrational wish to be remembered and regarded as important to the charity. A lot of the complaints about charities that one hears are based on these feelings that the complainant's efforts on behalf of the charity were not sufficiently valued. It is, of course, administratively difficult for a charity to individualize each appeal, and each receipt, and any such attempt founders without continuity of staff (or volunteers).

One important factor in maintaining an accurate record of past donors is that there can be a rapid turnover of a charity's staff, and the donor file will give some record of what has been done in the past. Nothing is more galling for a newly-appointed fund-raiser than to receive an irate letter from a donor protesting at a renewed appeal, for it makes him appear inefficient, whereas if no records have been kept he could not know.

Despite great efforts, it is unlikely that any charity will be able to keep its donor file completely up-to-date, and without duplication. Because of this, and the criticism it provokes from those receiving two or more copies of an appeal, charities often include in their mailings a specific message apologizing if duplication has taken place and asking the recipient to pass any spare copies of the appeal to a friend.

Keeping informed

All those working for charity will want up-to-date information on issues in their field, and on matters affecting charities. Apart from such crucial sources as the national and local press, charity fund-raisers should also be aware of other sources of information. The Charity Commissioners issue annual reports, which include a survey of legislation affecting charities, and of recent test cases, as well as general observations.

The National Council of Social Service provides a meeting place for those working in the social service field, both voluntary and professional. It keeps its members informed as to developments within their field which may concern them, as well as developments affecting charities in general. The NCSS acts as a spokesman on behalf of charities and a watchdog of their interests. It undertakes research on matters likely to interest charities, and aims to provide an information service at a more sophisticated and comprehensive level than could be undertaken by the individual charities without incurring high costs. Members are sent a newsletter ten times a year, and may also subscribe to *Look Europe*, which provides charities with information on EEC matters relevant to charities. The NCSS also publishes books and leaflets.

An organization wishing to join the NCSS should write in, outlining its aims (as set out in its trust deed), together with some general information on its work and including its latest annual report and set of audited accounts. A membership fee has recently been introduced, but the NCSS claim that genuine inability to pay would not mean an organization would be excluded. Each member organization is assigned to a special interest group (e.g. women, youth, community work) and will have an opportunity, through occasional meetings, to meet with others in the group, and will also receive occasional mailings from the group.

The NCSS is being increasingly regarded by officialdom as charity's spokesman and is used in this context more and more. For example, the applications for the grants from the European Poverty Programme (see pp. 133–4) were, in fact, made via a working party of the NCSS (though they did not have to be). Similarly, the NCSS appointed the trustees who determined the distribution of income from the first issue of the charity stamp. It is in a charity's interest to belong to the NCSS, so as to be kept informed on any issues of interest, and also so as to influence any decisions taken on behalf of charities.

The Charities Aid Foundation was founded by the NCSS and provides a range of valuable services to charities. It will undertake the administration of covenants on behalf of a charity, for a small fee. It operates a discretionary covenant scheme for companies and individuals (see p. 82), thus increasing the amounts available for distribution to charity. It publishes the *Directory of Grant-Making Trusts* (see p. 51), and holds periodic conferences and seminars on issues of interest to charities.

Conclusion

Something in excess of £200 million is donated to charities in the UK each year. The belief that there is one charity cake, with each charity competing for a larger slice for itself, is surely wrong, for surveys show that little over one-third of the adult population ever gives to charity. What we must strive to do is not only increase the amount given by each individual but also increase the numbers of those giving at all.

1 Groups

Groups of supporters are of great use to a charity—undertaking fund-raising, supporting pressure group activities, buying from the charity's trading operation, providing the personnel for flag days, gaining local publicity for the charity's work, and, all in all, helping to give the impression of dynamism and success, crucial to the charity. The fact that a charity has widespread support gives its pronouncements greater weight.

The type of groups can vary enormously. They can be geographically based or based on a trade or profession. They may be specifically for young people, or for students, or for either men or women only. They may be limited to a particular school or firm. They may be set up as temporary, ad hoc groups to deal with an apparent crisis, or they may be permanent, surviving changes of membership.

Although a charity can derive benefit from individual supporters, in the same way as from its groups, it should be recognized that the group performs a social function for its members and, if its members find it agreeable, will sustain their interest and preparedness to help the cause.

Affiliation to the parent organization

The group uses the charity's name, and care must be taken that it does not sully it. A charity's groups should be under the control of the parent body and must abide by its rules and regulations. Each new group should be required to be registered with the charity as an affiliated group. The affiliation form (issued by the charity) should clearly state the aims of the charity, and the chairman, secretary and treasurer of the group should sign an undertaking on the group's behalf to abide by the charity's constitution. A constitution to be adopted by its groups should be prepared by the charity, covering: the objects of the charity; the aims of the group; its affiliation to the charity; to whom membership is open; the regulations for an AGM; the election of officers and a committee and their functions; the control of funds; and the dissolution of the group. It shall also indicate a warning that any group may be disaffiliated if it fails to act in accordance with its affiliation agreement.

Contact with the groups

Apart from a charity's control of its groups through affiliation agreements, it is important to make sure that regular contact is maintained with all groups, as they can, through their use of the charity's name, mar its image. It is important that the group projects an image consistent with that of the charity. Both because of a need to keep an eye on its groups, and to encourage their activities, it is usual for the larger charities to appoint a national groups organizer, often with field staff throughout the regions.

Obviously, the necessity for such staff is determined by the number of groups it has, and the reliance it wants to put on groups within its overall campaign. In appointing a groups organizer great care must be taken—for he has the job of filling people with sufficient enthusiasm to undertake sometimes onerous work, and the organizer must be tactful enough to guide people's activities. If a group dislikes a person who is, in effect, the headquarters representative, then they quickly move on to carping about headquarters. It is usual for a charity to require its regional staff to undertake functions over and above servicing groups, such as overseeing thrift shops, or talking to schools in the area.

In drawing up the regulations for affiliation it is sensible for the parent organization to require its groups to send minutes of meetings to headquarters. Similarly, groups should be kept informed of headquarters activity. One way of doing this is to send the secretary of each group any press releases issued by headquarters. In some cases it might be considered proper to send the minutes of the meetings of the Executive Committee of the charity, but this depends on the closeness of the relationship with the groups, and the degree of confidentiality the Executive Committee likes to preserve. As a general rule, groups which fund-raise, but do not involve themselves in formulating the policies of the charity, do not need to be kept so closely in touch with policy decisions as those that wish to play an integral part in decision making.

How to form groups

Sometimes someone contacts the charity and says he wants to form a group. In this case, the first thing to do is to vet the person. It can damage the charity's image to have its cause espoused by, for example, the racially prejudiced or the religious bigot. If the charity has a groups organizer then it is his job to visit the person, or to invite him to headquarters. In a small charity the job could be undertaken by a voluntary worker. The person offering to form a group must be clear as to the charity's aims, and be sympathetic to them—he should not expect to change them. Whilst a charity should not look for uncritical devotion from its followers, beware the person who is seeking to infiltrate the organization to change it to his satisfaction. A charity should not be afraid of refusing help if it feels it is going to be detrimental to its cause.

The person proposing to start a group may have had previous experience of group organization, and need very little help, but more often people need a little guidance on how to set about launching the group. The same procedure can be followed if there has been a request to start a group in an area, or if a charity's staff decide to launch a group in an area.

1. The group's working area must be decided (whether it is to be geographically defined or limited by occupation). The geographical area chosen should be small rather than large—because the group should be able to cover its chosen area effectively. If it chooses a large area it inhibits the establishment of other groups within its area.

2. Planning a launching meeting. This can be held in a private house or a public hall. The hall hired should not be too large—anticipate an audience of 30–40 people. It should be convenient for public transport and preferably non-sectarian. The date chosen should not coincide with some popular television programme or local community event, and the time of the meeting should allow people sufficient time to dine after returning home from work.

3. Contacting contacts. Any donors in the area (whose names should be recorded on the donor file, see pp. 16–17) should be con-

tacted and invited to join the group being formed in the area, and invited to the meeting.

4. Local organizations, such as Rotary, youth groups, women's clubs and political parties should be notified of the start of the group.

5. Publicity. The impending launch of the group must be publicized as much as possible. Posters advertising the meeting—preferably including the name and phone number of someone to be contacted for people who might like to join the group but cannot attend the meeting—should be prominently displayed, for example, in shop windows, the local library, etc., for up to four weeks in advance. It is useful for a national charity to be able to supply 'blank' posters, which bear the charity's name, and leave space for details of a meeting to be filled in. If there is time, and sufficient manpower, leaflets inviting people to join the group, and attend the launching meeting, can be delivered house-to-house, or handed out at busy street corners: this should be about a week before the meeting. A letter should be sent to the local papers, inviting people to join the group. Press releases about the launching meeting should be sent to the local press, and local radio and television stations.

The launching meeting

It is important that the meeting projects an image of a lively, go-ahead charity, with which people would like to be associated. To make the meeting interesting and attract a bigger audience it is sensible to show a film on the charity's work (if there is one) or to have a well-known speaker to talk about the charity. There should be a chairman who welcomes the audience, introduces and thanks the speakers and summarizes the proceedings, by inviting the audience to join the new group being formed to help the work of the charity. The choice of chairman is crucial—he can make or break the meeting. He must be a good public speaker, and attractive to the audience. If the group is likely to be drawn mostly from students, then avoid a paternalistic chairman who might be excellent for a more conservative group. If a good local chairman cannot be found then the charity should send out one of its headquarters staff or one of its trustees.

If there is already a nucleus of a group in an area, and the launching meeting is an attempt to increase numbers, then the chairman can invite the audience to support the temporary appointment of officers—chairman, secretary and treasurer—who will act until the members know each other better and proper elections can be held. Or the chairman can ask for volunteers for these jobs on a temporary basis. It is important to have some organization established at this first meeting and to fix a date for a second meeting at which the group can discuss and decide on its programme.

The launching meeting should make people want to join, enable them to do so and fire them with enthusiasm for the cause. Members should be signed up at the meeting—with proper cards, and receipts issued. The meeting can be asked to decide on how much membership should cost.

How the group should be organized

All groups should be affiliated to the parent body. Some charities like their groups to be organized to a standard pattern, others do not particularly care and allow groups to evolve the organization most suitable to themselves. Usually, a group finds it useful to elect certain of its members to serve on a committee and to undertake specific tasks. The chairman sees that all tasks are carried out as promised, is the spokesman for the local group and chairs meetings. The secretary notifies members of meetings, keeps minutes, deals with correspondence and is responsible for keeping an up-to-date list of members. The treasurer is responsible for the group's funds. He must keep an accurate record of all expenditure and receipts and is responsible for collection of membership fees. The publicity and press officer is responsible for producing posters and leaflets and getting them distributed and for sending out press notices. An education officer may be useful for recruiting support in schools and colleges. Other officers can be appointed as found necessary, such as a membership secretary, vice-chairman or minutes secretary. All officers should be active: there is no point in having figureheads as officers—call them President and Vice-President. A genial, cheerful and efficient committee is of inestimable value to a group, for it avoids the internal rows and ill-feeling that committee work seems to generate.

The group should hold regular meetings, at least one a month. It is important that the group does not divide itself into committee members and the rest, so that ordinary members feel left out of things and that their opinions do not count. At the group's meetings all members should be able to contribute their opinions. Meetings should be held to decide what to do—not to waste time. Minutes must be kept to show who committed themselves to what action. The circulation of the minutes often acts as a timely reminder to all concerned, and at each meeting the responsible person should report on the progress that has been made in fulfilling the wishes of the last meeting. To deal with specific events, such as a bazaar or a street collection, the group may find it useful to appoint a special sub-committee. The sub-committee should have a well-defined task, and must report regularly back to the group as a whole.

An annual general meeting should be held by the group, and a brief report on the year's activities, together with a statement of accounts, circulated to all members before the meeting. It may be sensible to combine this with the charity's annual report, to save postage and to remind the group's members that their work is part of the whole. The election of officers should be made at the AGM.

What the group should do

The group is not simply a social club—it exists to help the charity. It may do this primarily by fund-raising, but also by local campaigning on the charity's behalf. Some supporters enjoy fund-raising, others shy away from it—but groups must be reminded that the need for funds is central to the charity's existence, and that their success or failure as fund-raisers affects those in dire need.

Groups should organize the type of fund-raising activity suitable for its members and the area in which it operates. The group should be warned to avoid like poison events where they have to lay out large sums of money, because in this case money can be lost, not simply not made. Also they should not assume that, because there are no dances or concerts or whist drives in their area, there is a huge, unsatisfied demand: on the contrary, it may mean that there is not sufficient demand.

The group should know how to plan and cost an event. The costing involves writing down all the likely costs which will be incurred, and then balancing them against the likely receipts. It should also be considered whether the likely net profit is large enough to warrant the effort (for time can always be spent house-to-house collecting, for guaranteed results).

The group should not muscle-in on any areas of fund-raising

that should be centralized, most notably appeals to trusts or national industry. Fund-raising of this type should be undertaken in conjunction with headquarters staff. Nothing is more galling than finding a group has secured a £5 donation from a firm which could have been expected to give £100 to a national appeal, and which, when re-approached, argues that it has already given. The charity should make clear to its groups if there is any type of fund-raising it does not want its groups to do.

There is an enormous range of fund-raising activities which groups can undertake and the choice must rest with the members.

Flag days and house-to-house collections

Each group should have one flag day and one house-to-house collection a year. Not only is the money raised useful, but such events also attract publicity. If the group has not got enough members to cover the whole of its area, it can join with another charity's local group, and share a flag-day permit, or can cover only part of its area in a house-to-house collection.

For information on organizing flag days and house-to-house collections, see Chapter 6.

Carol singing

The group should either go carol singing with its own members, or try to recruit local choirs to sing for the charity.

For the organization of carol singing, see Chapter 2, p. 45.

Sponsored events

There are dozens of types of events which can be sponsored, ranging from the familiar sponsored walk to sponsored work-ins and silences. They are particularly popular with younger members of the group.

For the organization of sponsored events, see Chapter 2, pp. 41–5.

Sale of the charity's Christmas cards

The group should be encouraged to sell the charity's Christmas cards (and other goods supplied by the charity's trading subsidiary) to friends, relations and business colleagues. Goods can be sold through the charity's catalogue, if there is one, or from samples obtained from the charity's headquarters or at bring-and-buy sales, coffee mornings and bazaars. Sales of Christmas cards should be started early in the season—September or October.

Stunts

Penny miles, pancake races, tiddly winks competitions can all help to attract publicity for the charity's work, and be linked with fund-raising events such as street collections.

Jumble sales

There is a real demand for jumble in many areas and jumble sales raise useful sums of money. The jumble sale should be held in a local church hall or school hall, which is usually used for such events (the local newspaper will show where other charities hold their jumble sales). Visit a few halls and see which seems the best. Choose a date which does not clash with any other important local events, or holidays, and make sure it is convenient for most members. Book the hall well in advance, so that you can be sure of securing the desired date.

To collect things for sale, group members should ask friends and family for good quality jumble. The main categories of saleable jumble are clothes, especially children's, books and records, bric-a-brac and toys. Much the biggest demand is for good quality every-day clothes. If the group's members do not collect enough jumble amongst themselves, then a small advertisement asking for jumble and giving details of the sale can be placed in the local news-paper. The advertisement should include a telephone number to ring, to arrange collection.

The jumble should be sorted out ruthlessly before the sale. A member's garage is an ideal place to do this, and to store the jumble in. All items offered for sale should be in good condition. If you would be insulted by being offered any item, do not offer it to others. Price things cheaply. It is better to shift everything at a low price, rather than have piles of goods left over, and a subsequent disposal problem. If a tweed skirt cost £6 new and is scarcely worn, do not be tempted to price it at £3—the person buying at jumble sales knows where to buy a new skirt, though of poorer quality, for £2, so price the skirt at 75p or at the most £1. Remember, all the goods were donated, so after paying for the hire of the hall and any advertising, any money received is profit.

If large quantities of clothing of outstandingly good quality, which has been scarcely worn, are collected, then consider holding a 'good as new' sale. This is not another name for a jumble sale, but signifies a sale of better quality items. It will attract customers prepared to pay higher prices than for jumble, but expecting garments which really are as good as new. It damages the charity's image to give the impression of cheating the public.

If when sorting the jumble items are found, especially in the bric-a-brac category, which are of real value, then they should be put aside for a bazaar or antique sale, where a higher price can be charged. But try to include some interesting articles in the jumble sale, to encourage local antique hunters who may spend money on refreshments or donate to the charity or buy from the home-made produce stall. Jumble sales attract two different types of customer. The first is seeking out second-hand clothing, and for them the jumble sale is a real service. The second category is the browser, hoping to spot a Staffordshire figure for 5p. You will learn from experience whether the first or second category is the more profitable in your area. To cater for the first, one simply needs good quality jumble. To take money from the browsers one should try to expand the bric-a-brac section, have a home-made goods stall (selling chutneys, marmalades, cakes, scones, etc.), perhaps have a plant stall selling plants grown by members. Again, all items should be priced low. If possible, serve refreshments—tea, soft drinks, home-made cakes and biscuits.

Advertise the sale by an advertisement in the local newspaper, perhaps in the two issues preceding the sale. Try a letter to the newspaper from a well-known person, urging people to support the sale and cause (for a small jumble sale this is not necessary, but for a big, annual sale it might be worth while). Posters advertising the sale should be put up in local shops and, if the size of the sale warrants the effort, duplicated handbills can be distributed door-to-door.

It is unlikely that every single item will be sold. Either arrange for one of the group's members to store the left-over jumble for the next sale or, if this is not practicable or some of the items seem unsaleable at any future event, then arrange for a used clothes dealer to take them away. Make the arrangement provisionally before the sale so that the dealer can come to clear the hall the same afternoon.

Bazaars

These may have a 'good as new' or a 'jumble' stall, but will specialize in hand-made goods and have side-shows. Choosing a suitable hall and a suitable date are the same as for a jumble sale, and the same methods of obtaining publicity should be used. Because a bazaar is more of an occasion than a jumble sale, a personality can be invited to open it. It is a good idea to devise a theme for the bazaar. If it is near Easter then it can be an Easter Fair which, in addition to the usual stalls, could sell bulbs and spring flowers, Easter eggs, simnel cake and hot cross buns. A Christmas Fair will, of course, have Christmas cards and calendars, Christmas puddings and mince pies, masses of suitable presents and perhaps a Father Christmas. Apart from seasonal themes one can devise bazaars based on foreign countries—like a French fair, with the refreshment stall set out as a café, and the home-made goods stall selling quiches and mousses; or a Dutch fair, with a cheese stall and bulbs. To be honest, most of the goods on sale will be the same, whatever the theme of the bazaar, but it creates a jolly atmosphere, and attracts customers. To decorate a hall suitably for a bazaar with a foreign theme, ask the tourist office of the country involved to supply posters. Some national costumes, and costumes for clowns and Easter rabbits and Father Christmas outfits can be hired from Barnums, 67 Hammersmith Road, London W14. A Toy Fair, which has mostly toys, although some other traditional bazaar items, can be a great success, especially if held around October and November, when people are looking for Christmas presents.

A significant proportion of the money taken at bazaars is from competitions and games—such as coconut shies, guessing the weight of the cake, hoopla, crockery smashing, raffles, bran tubs and tombolas. Depending on the size of the hall, and the interests of the helpers, the following stalls can be part of the bazaar:

refreshment stall	—can serve teas, soft drinks, also jacket potatoes, ice cream, hot dogs.
home-made goods	—jams, marmalades, chutneys, cakes, breads.
home-sewn goods	—especially baby clothes, small gift items such as aprons, lavender bags, embroidered tray cloths, tablecloths.
stamp collectors' corner	—mixed bags of foreign and British stamps, as well as more valuable individual items.

book and record stall	—second-hand books and records.
good as new clothing	—if sufficient quantities divide into children's, men's and women's, and have three stalls.
bottle stall	—a bottle tombola (bottles can vary from tomato ketchup to sherry). All bottles are numbered, and tickets sold are of equal value, though the bottle prizes vary in worth. Not all tickets need have winning numbers.
tombola	—run on the same principle as the bottle stall, but with various gifts.
bric-a-brac stall	—small items, antique if possible, but can include new jewellery. Household and larger items are best sold separately, perhaps on a white elephant stall.
groceries	—donated tinned and packaged food.
toy stall	—can include children's books.
plant and flower stall	

If the charity has a trading subsidiary then there should be a stall selling its goods and cards.

To increase the number of goods for sale, and to offer as tombola or raffle prizes, approach local shops and manufacturers for gifts. Most are used to such requests and will try to find something of use.

Christine Fagg's book, *Raise Cash, Have Fun* (Elek), lists many ideas for competitions and side shows suitable for bazaars. There is nothing to stop a group organizing sales of books or records or plants, rather than selling a variety of goods, but the sale with a variety of goods will attract more customers, and is a good way of hedging one's bets.

A successful bazaar will become known throughout the area, and remembered as a good place to spot bargains, as well as affording a good afternoon's entertainment for the family.

Fêtes

These are like bazaars, but held out of doors. As for all outdoor activities, their success depends largely on the weather. It is possible to insure against rain through the Pluvius Insurance scheme of the Eagle Insurance Company. Fêtes can be held in someone's large garden or on a village green or in school grounds. Try to find a place which people would like to visit for its own sake, like a grand country house or a beautiful garden. The outdoor aspect can be exploited by having energetic competitions like bowling for a pig and fishing for champagne bottles, as well as attractions such as maypole dancing. The central event of the fête can be a donkey derby, a series of donkey races. There can be a tote, although someone with experience would be needed to run it successfully. For a donkey derby a good public address system is essential, as is a good commentator—try a local radio station for a disc jockey. The information necessary to follow the derby is an ideal way of selling a programme (see Chapter 4, p. 63).

Social events—coffee mornings, wine and cheese parties

These are most usually relatively small-scale events held in a member's house. They help maintain the group's friendly atmosphere as well as raising funds. Members bring friends and family and a modest admission charge is made which may include the cost of the refreshments. Increased profits are yielded if a bring-and-buy sale or a raffle is held in conjunction with the event. Because they require little organization, coffee mornings, wine and cheese parties or coffee evenings can be held at regular intervals—if members like them.

Barbecues

The same risk of bad weather spoiling the event applies to barbecues as to any outdoor event. An insurance policy against rain should be considered, especially if a great deal of effort and some money have been expended. The food is, of course, the central feature of the barbecue, but it may be combined with a dance. The event can be held in a large garden, but usually a field hired or borrowed from a sympathetic farmer is more practicable. Make sure that it is accessible and that there are car parking facilities.

If the barbecue is not just limited to a small cook-in in a member's garden, then a great deal of prior publicity is needed. Print car stickers and try to get them displayed as widely as possible for three or four weeks before the event. If you are planning to roast a whole pig, or ox, write to the local press and tell them. Place an advertisement in the local paper. Prior publicity is important, so that as many tickets as possible can be sold in advance, which enables more accurate catering, cutting down on costly waste, and also means that if the weather is not too good people will not be deterred. The food to serve is sausages, jacket potatoes, barbecued meats and baked beans. The admission ticket may cover the cost of food, or part of it—say one portion with additional portions on sale. Heap the plates up, so that people feel they are getting good value—their good humour will be shown in their support of the side shows and stalls. If you have a friendly licensee you can run a bar, but cider needs no licence, nor, of course, do soft drinks

You can have stalls and sell goods at a barbecue, and have side shows, preferably with an outdoor theme, like bobbin' apples or bowling for a pig. It is always a good idea to have a raffle and/or tombola at any social event for charity.

A barbecue can be great fun. The main points to watch are that the location is accessible, that publicity is widespread and that sufficient tickets can be sold in advance to make a profit. Before embarking on a barbecue, or any other large-scale function, the members of the group should each guarantee to sell a certain number of tickets; if the number each can guarantee to sell is not sufficient to cover all costs, then the group should not go forward with the planned event. The tickets sold to members of the public as a result of the publicity are the profit, together with the proceeds of the side shows and stalls.

Guy Fawkes party

This follows much the same planning principles as a barbecue, except that the firework display, not the food, is central to the evening. The prior publicity should include a story to the local paper announcing that the group's firework party is designed to provide a safe way for children and others to enjoy the fireworks. That said, make sure that it is, in fact, safe. It is best held in a large garden, as people will not want to travel out into the country in November. Charge a modest admission fee. If enough people are expected, so that the costs are covered, contact one of the large firework manufacturers and have a custom-built display. The admission charges should cover the cost of the fireworks; the profit should come from the sale of hot drinks, jacket potatoes, soup, hot dogs, sausages, toffee apples, treacle toffee, etc. On a cold November evening, people are very ready to buy hot snacks. Hold a raffle. If facilities permit it, there can be an indoor party after the bonfire and fireworks have burnt themselves out. In this case there can be some stalls with items for sale.

Re-cycling collections

A range of household articles can be sold for re-cycling. These include paper, bottles, wool, aluminium, cotton, lead, egg cartons. The collections can be short or long term, but the markets for all re-cyclable materials fluctuate widely over quite short periods of time, so that it is difficult to plan long term collections, and rely on the income, as the market can collapse (as happened in 1975 with waste paper).

The first stage is to decide what to collect. Paper can be sold to local waste paper merchants, listed in the Yellow Pages. If none are listed then the Paper and Board Manufacturers Federation will give the name of the nearest member. Paper is in plentiful supply, so it is not hard to come by it, but its bulk provides problems. It should be kept dry—if possible store it in somebody's garage or the local church hall. The large waste paper merchants will lend, free of charge, fire proof containers, which will hold five tonnes of paper. The paper merchant will tell you if he wants different types of paper sorted separately. Books are usually acceptable. Most paper merchants will collect (usually a minimum of one tonne) and if your local merchant refuses then the Paper and Board Manufacturers Federation will probably be able to tell you one who will. When there is a shortage of waste paper, as in 1974, waste paper merchants are surprisingly obliging; but when the market slumps, as in 1975, they are reluctant to buy paper, let alone collect it!

Let people in the area know that the group will be collecting paper a week or two in advance and ask them to save it for you. Publicize the collection by a letter to the local press, a press release and a stunt—have a personality collect paper and invite a photographer from the local paper to witness the event. You must be reliable! If you have undertaken to collect the paper you must do so, or you will lose goodwill for the cause. Do not take on the commitment of collecting paper week after week if group members are not prepared to sustain the effort. Additional collectors can be recruited from the local Friends of the Earth or Conservation Society, or the local youth groups, if necessary on a profit sharing basis.

The procedure for collecting other items for re-cycling is roughly similar to waste paper collection. Always find a dealer who will buy your scrap before you start to collect it. Make sure that you have adequate storage space, and publicize your scheme well. Try to find local merchants, as the nearer the depot the higher the price. If you cannot find a local merchant to buy the commodity you wish to collect, then it is worth contacting the appropriate Trade Association. Do not rely on re-cycled goods for a constant income, as the market for them fluctuates widely.

Collecting trading stamps, postage stamps and coins

Trading stamp companies—Green Shield, Co-operative Societies and Pink Stamps—all operate charity schemes, and will redeem stamps for either cash or goods. Charities have purchased ambulances, school or sports equipment through the schemes.

To organize a trading stamps collection, first make sure that people know that the charity is collecting them. If it is for a specific purpose, then send the story to the local newspaper, including an address to which they may be sent. Put up posters asking for trading stamps, ideally in the supermarkets and petrol stations in which they are given, and provide a box into which the stamps can be placed. The trading stamp companies themselves provide some promotional material free of charge, such as charts, posters and boxes.

Postage stamps can be collected and sold to local stamp dealers. Shop around to see who offers the best prices. Not only unusual stamps, but also ordinary, everyday, British ones have a re-sale value, in quantity. To bolster the collection of stamps, produce a small poster 'We could use your used stamps' and giving brief details of the charity's work and where to send the stamps, or whom to contact for collection. Ask local shops and post offices to display the posters. Ask shops and offices which are likely to receive a lot of post, such as travel agents or solicitors, to save the stamps for you, at least for a few weeks. Consider offering a small prize to the local youth group or school which collects the most stamps for your cause.

Coins, both foreign and British pre-decimal, can be collected in the same way. Ask local banks to display posters appealing for left-over change from foreign holidays—which the bank will not change, but for which a coin dealer should give face value.

Raffles

Held in conjunction with a social event, or simply on its own, a raffle can be a good source of income. Some people object to raffles as a form of gambling, and this may be true of group members. It is not worth losing supporters for the sake of holding a raffle, so sound out feeling before committing the group to holding the raffle. Stringent legal regulations must be complied with. These are, briefly:

1. A lottery will be one of three types: (a) a small lottery, incidental to another entertainment such as a dance or bazaar; (b) a private lottery in which tickets are sold only to group members; (c) a public lottery, when tickets can be sold to the public.
2. Regulations for small lotteries: the proceeds, other than permitted expenses, must go to the charity. The permitted expenses are the cost of printing the raffle tickets and a sum up to £50 for prizes. The prizes may not be money prizes. The sale of tickets and the draw and announcement of the result must take place on the premises in which the entertainment (to which the lottery is incidental) takes place, during its progress. Money cannot be refunded on a ticket (this applies to all lotteries).
3. Regulations for private lotteries: tickets must be printed, with the price marked, and bearing the name and address of the promoters. It must also show that the sale of tickets is restricted to members and that the prize will be delivered only to the winner. The proceeds of the raffle must go to the charity or can go in prizes (this is after allowed expenses for printing). The raffle may not be advertised, other than the advertisement on the ticket, except on the premises of the charity, or those of the promoter. Tickets must not be sent through the post.
4. Regulations for public lotteries: the charity, or its affiliated group, must register with the local authority. A public lottery may be held only by a registered charity or an organization that can be shown to benefit society as a whole. The promoters of the lottery must be members of the charity and authorized by its officers to act as promoters. The promoter must not be paid for organizing the lottery. No prize may exceed £1,000, and no single ticket may cost more than 25p. The proceeds – after allowed expenses for printing and prizes –

must go to the charity. The expenses may not exceed 25 per cent of the proceeds. The amount spent on prizes must not exceed 50 per cent of the whole proceeds. The total value of tickets sold must not exceed £5,000, and no lotteries may be organized by the same society at the same time at which the total value of the tickets sold is greater than £10,000. Advertising the lottery must be limited to a notice in the premises of the charity or in literature distributed only to members. Every ticket must show the price of the ticket, the name and address of the promoter, the name of the charity and the date of the draw. Tickets must not be sent through the post to non-members. The costs of the lottery (expenses and prizes) must come from its proceeds, not from the general income of the charity (though if the lottery is a dismal failure and a loss is made it is not an offence). No one under sixteen can buy or sell a lottery ticket. The lottery promoter must send a return to the local authority, showing the proceeds, the deductions of expenses and prizes, the dates between which the tickets were sold, and how the proceeds are to be applied. The return form must be certified by two other members of the Society, so authorized by its governing body, and both over twenty-one.

Full details of the law on lotteries are given in *Voluntary Organizations and the Law relating to Lotteries and Gaming* (NCSS). It is clear that these regulations are honoured more in their breach than in their observance. The Home Office is currently re-examining the regulations for lotteries. Occasionally, token prosecutions are brought.

To hold a successful raffle, you need good prizes to tempt people to try their luck, and willing ticket sellers. Although the law allows the purchase of prizes, it is much better to have them donated. Try local shopkeepers, travel agents and garages. Try not to have just a few, big prizes, but also a large number of small ones. People will buy your raffle tickets again if they won last time, or if they know someone else who did. Each group member should be given a minimum number of tickets to sell, for which they are responsible (the implication being that they buy, themselves, those that they are unable to sell). Tickets should be sold to friends, colleagues, family and neighbours. Some people like to take a gamble, so enjoy buying raffle tickets—often those selling the tickets forget this and see themselves as pushing unwanted goods. Make sure that all the ticket stubs are returned in good time for the draw. If this is held at a social event, such as a bazaar or dance, do not forget to sell the tickets during the event; the display of prizes should increase interest. Send details of the winners' names to the local paper—it brings the name of the charity before the public.

Summary

A charity's groups can raise money for its cause in a myriad of ways. The choice of method should reflect members' interests and their experience. Care should be taken not to be over-ambitious and risk losing funds on expensive deposits or hiring fees. Group fund-raising should be both enjoyable and profitable, so that members maintain their enthusiasm. Some groups welcome guidance from the charity's headquarters on fund-raising, others resent it, so care and discretion must be exercised by the charity's staff when dealing with its groups.

2 Schools and youth groups

There is in Britain a tradition of using children as fund-raisers, and many major national charities employ more than a dozen people to work in schools, furthering their cause. The least attractive aspect of charity fund-raising in schools—though the least trouble to the charity—is when the school announces that a collection will be held at assembly the next day and the parent has to provide the donation. This points to inequalities of wealth and generosity, neither of them the child's fault, and makes them feel responsible for the actions of their parents. The best form of fund-raising in schools is where the children earn the money, and where enthusiasm counts more than parental wealth, and where the children learn to be sympathetic to the charity's beneficiaries. It is more useful in the long run if children learn to overcome their prejudices about the handicapped, the poor and the sick rather than retain their antipathies and raise money for them. This should be remembered in all charity work with young people.

How to approach schools and youth groups

The addresses of secondary schools in the UK can be found in the *Education Authorities Directory* (The School Government Publishing Company). Boys' public schools are listed in the *Public and Preparatory Schools Year Book* (Black) and girls' public schools are listed in the *Girls' School Year Book* (Black). Catholic schools are listed in *Catholic Education: A Handbook* (available from the Catholic Council for England and Wales, 41 Cromwell Road, London SW7). No list of primary schools for the whole country is published. Lists of schools for individual areas can be obtained from the Education Officer of that district. Some refuse to give the list to charities, maintaining that no material may be sent direct to the school—a policy they can scarcely hope to enforce. The School Government Publishing Company, Darby House, Bletchingley Road, Merstham, Redhill, Surrey, undertakes mailings to primary or secondary schools and other educational establishments.

A comprehensive list of youth groups can be found in the *Year Book of the Youth Service in England and Wales* (Youth Service Information Centre). Many youth organizations mail their constituent member clubs regularly and, if given enough notice, will include a letter from a charity with a mailing, thus saving the charity postal costs. The charity should offer to pay any marginal postage costs—if its material adds weight, so making each letter dearer. Several months' notice may be needed by the organizations, so allow plenty of time.

In schools, headteachers or teachers are the key figures—there are not many campaigns that are led from the bottom in schools. The type of approach to the school will depend on the size of the campaign to be launched. There are approximately 38,000 schools in the UK and a charity can, if it likes, mail all of them, or can concentrate on one area or type of school.

If mailing to schools, remember that a great number of people are sending literature into schools and the headteacher may respond by throwing it into the wastepaper basket, especially if it is a circular letter. A telephone call follow-up, or an individual (as opposed to a circular) letter will increase the response rate, but involves a large amount of work, and therefore staff time.

As it is unlikely in a mass mailing to schools that each letter can be individually 'topped and tailed', because of the numbers involved, it is often better to try and get the letter signed by a celebrity. It seems more acceptable to get a circular letter from someone famous than from someone unknown. Although it is the headteacher or youth club leader who will initially decide on whether or not to take part in the campaign, it is important that the children view the prospect with enthusiasm. So try to select a celebrity attractive to both children and teachers and youth club leaders—wholesome comedians and pious pop stars are usual. (For information on how to contact celebrities, see p. 106.)

Letters which are simple requests for money are least likely to succeed—generally, headteachers do not like to hold collections in their schools except for disasters. The best letters are those in which the school is invited to take part in a campaign, and ways of raising money are suggested: these can range from carol singing to waste paper collection or sponsored work schemes. When writing to schools, enclose a letter to the pupils and ask the headteacher to read it at morning assembly. Include a tear-off slip on the letter to the headteacher, to show that fairly prompt action is required. Invite the school or youth club to write for further information, badges, posters, and, if you can supply one, for a speaker.

Youth clubs are a more difficult target to approach than schools, because the leaders are often more transient, and so it is hard to build up a committed body of support. Also the clubs are often in need of funds themselves. When writing to youth clubs, only one letter, addressed 'Dear Friends', is necessary, as it is most usually pinned up on the notice board for members to read.

If your charity has an especially novel or worthy scheme for raising money in schools, then it is worth trying to obtain the endorsement of the local Education Officer or Mayor. Local education authorities are generally cautious about encouraging charities to fund-raise in schools, well aware that they are likely to be criticized by rival charities, the miserly and those who genuinely object to the use of children as fund-raisers. But occasionally an Education Officer, or more usually the local Mayor, can be coaxed into sending a covering letter of the 'I hope you can lend your support to this worthy cause' type. Such endorsements are of great value.

If you are sending a speaker into a school or youth club, try to get someone attractive to young people. People in their twenties are generally better than those in their fifties, who will seem too like teachers. Children respond to enthusiasm and not to lecturing. They are prepared to be entertained by the speaker—a welcome diversion from lessons—so try to make the talk lively. Often too long a time is allowed—even an hour and a half—and the most capable speaker will find his voice becomes automatic, his ideas exhausted. If the time allowed to the speaker is longer than twenty minutes, then consider showing a film, or slides, or passing round samples, or playing appropriate records. In other words, recognize that the human voice begins to drone after twenty minutes.

When a school or youth club agrees to help, then it helps them if ideas for fund-raising can be given, and also if incentives such as badges are offered. Charts showing the progress of their efforts are a help—an easy one to design is in the form of a thermometer.

Competitions

Sometimes children respond well to competitions, for example, one to see which school collects the most waste paper or money, or devises the best poster or fund-raising idea. Prizes can be of value—for example, £250 of school equipment to be chosen by the headteacher, or a foreign holiday for an individual prizewinner—or it can be a token, such as a certificate. The prize can be offered to the institution or the individual. If offering a valuable prize, the charity should persuade a firm to give it, rather than use its own funds.

Some people find the offer of a reward to children for their charity efforts to be objectionable. Competitions are objectionable if they do not present equal chance of success to all sections of the community, and favour the richer child above the poor. But the poor child is as able to collect waste paper as the rich one, though perhaps not able to secure sponsors for a sponsored walk. But schools in poor areas may be more successful at raising money through jumble sales than those in well-to-do areas. It is important when devising a competition to be as fair as possible, and to make it interesting, so that people want to take part.

Educational material

Whilst a charity may regard schoolchildren as fund-raising fodder, it must realize that headteachers do not share this attitude, and will be resentful of it. Fund-raising in schools should be of some educational benefit—if only making children aware of the problems of their world. To treat schools only as sources of funds is short-sighted—for today's young grow up to be the supporters of tomorrow (interestingly, people retain preferences for charities which they have known in their youth, so legacy income, for example, is relatively high for charities which are often past their peak in performance, need or popularity).

Apart from the sympathy which an educational programme by a charity can generate, which will ultimately lead to increased donations, every charity should remember that if public sympathy with its cause were sufficiently large then the charity's work might be rendered redundant by the government's assuming financial responsibility. Educational work should not be casually undertaken—it needs careful planning and thought. Modern techniques should be used wherever appropriate—such as simulation games, debates and teach-ins.

Groups in schools and colleges

In some cases it is possible to establish a continuing relationship with a school, youth club or college, and to formalize it by affiliating it to the parent body, as a group. (See pp. 19–20 on group affiliation.) Usually such continuous support depends on the enthusiasm of one member of staff, although if the school or college supports a charity for a number of years they can be encouraged to regard the relationship as 'traditional'.

A group at a school, college or university should be serviced by the charity's staff as one of its groups. Speakers should be offered, to make sure that enthusiasm is not allowed to flag.

Ideas for fund-raising suitable for young people

Some of these methods are suitable for both young and old. The general points on fund-raising in the chapters on groups and functions should be consulted.

Sponsored events

Anything can be sponsored—walking, sitting, dancing, not talking, carol singing, fasting and, perhaps most useful of all, working on some socially desirable project. The main principle is the same—the participant persuades people—usually family, friends or colleagues—to pay a specific amount per hour or mile. The success of sponsored events does not depend simply on how well they are organized or how many people take part, but rather on how many sponsors each of the participants manages to collect, and their generosity. People have been known to walk fifteen miles to collect the magnificent sum of 45p. Their time could have been better spent collecting house-to-house. So, in organizing a sponsored event, emphasize to participants the importance of getting sponsors.

Prepare an official sponsorship form, and make sure that each participant has one in good time to collect sufficient sponsors. Allow about four weeks. If planning a large-scale event with hundreds of participants, allow more time.

SPECIMEN SPONSORSHIP FORM:
Name of charity

Name of participant . . . .

Address . . . .

. . . .

Sponsored by:

Name and address of sponsor	Amount sponsored per mile

The above participant walked . . . . . miles in aid of

(charity's name). Signed . . . . Official steward.

The method of getting participants varies: if it is in a village or small town then posters and a letter to the local newspaper inviting participants should bring results, especially if backed up by approaches to local schools and youth clubs. Sometimes a single school or club organizes a sponsored event, with its members participating. If the charity is trying to organize a larger event—perhaps a nationwide day of fasting—then circularize the most likely sources of participants. Divide the country into areas, and put one person in charge of each area, responsible for organizing the event there. Remember older people will often join young people on walks or other events, so do not forget to inform adult organizations in the area that the event is taking place and that their support as either participants or sponsors would be welcome.

Surprising and disgusting as it may be, it is usual for participants to have problems collecting all the money pledged by sponsors. People do not always realize that 10p a lap round the football pitch can cost them £1.80 as a result of a diligent eight-year-old's efforts. Make sure that sponsors know roughly how much they are likely to have to pay out. Tell participants to collect the money as soon as possible after the event, when memories of commitment are fresh. But the charity should be prepared for disappointments.

Sponsored walks: When organizing walks, use common sense. Choose a safe route, round a park or school playing fields. The Ramblers Association will help you to plan a cross country route. If your route is on roads, check it with the police, inviting their suggestions for improving safety. Once the planned route has police approval, mention it on publicity, as it will reassure parents. Do not organize walks at night, or ones likely to last after the light fails. Make sure that both starting and finishing points are convenient for public transport, and have car-parking space.

As well as the sponsorship form, participants should be given in advance a sheet of instructions, showing the route, with checkpoints and lavatories marked, giving hints on road usage (walk singly on the right-hand side of the road, or if in a column then on the left-hand side), instructions to wear sensible shoes, and reminding them not to forget their sponsorship form. It can also include details on how to collect the money and where to send it. Make sure that all the walkers have the name, address and phone number of the main organizers in case there are any queries, and an emergency number to ring when on the walk, in case of difficulties.

Remember, the walkers are your responsibility: do not lose them. Have marshals to supervise the walkers, making sure that they behave sensibly. The marshals check-in the walkers at the start, patrol the route in cars, rescuing the drop-outs and handing out food and drink, providing first aid if necessary and check that all walkers pass the checkpoints on the route. All walkers should have badges, which make them conspicuous to the marshals, and also gain publicity. Unless you have a licence for a street collection on the day of the walk, then participants are not permitted to carry collecting boxes. For publicity purposes, it is worth having a gimmick, such as a walk in fancy dress, or with a celebrity starting it off, or with babies in prams.

Sponsored silences: Many parents are particularly ready to sponsor silences—especially if combined with study. The sponsorship could be made for every fifteen minutes (ten minutes if the participants are under eleven). It is the job of the supervisors, the equivalent of the walk's marshals, to register the participants, clock them in, ensure that there is no whispering, clock them off and sign their sponsorship forms. A defaulting participant is disqualified for the quarter of an hour in which he speaks, but can continue subsequently. It is often best to hold the silence at a school hall or youth club or community centre. Invite members of the public to come and gaze disbelievingly, and invite them to contribute.

Sponsored fasts: Fasts are good publicity-gaining events, especially when held out of doors on a market square, pedestrian precinct or some other public place. Though it is hard to attract large numbers to participate in this sort of event, those who do are usually highly motivated and can collect large numbers of sponsors. To increase the effectiveness of the fast, hold it on an appropriate day, such as United Nations Day for an overseas aid charity, or Armistice Day for charities for the war disabled. If no date seems particularly relevant to the cause, then choose Easter.

If fasting out of doors, then make sure that participants are warm—provide blankets and waterproof covering. They are not expected to fast completely, and can be given hot drinks. Do not make the fast so long that they will collapse: twelve or fourteen hours is unlikely to hurt anyone. Make the unit of sponsorship a quarter or half hour. Though the number of participants is likely to be small, they should still be supervised. Do not forget to inform the press: a picture of shivering, fasting people is likely to be popular with the papers.

Sponsored swims: These are like sponsored walks, except that the problems of supervision are localized, as all the participants will swim at one or two pools. Make sure that the marshals can life-save in case any rescue work is needed. Have hot drinks available for the swimmers. The unit of sponsorship is usually a length of the pool, but for small children fix the distances in widths, not lengths.

Sponsored fund-raising: With sponsored fund-raising, the charity can gain twice, once through the sponsorship money and once through the funds collected by participants. Carol singing, house-to-house collecting and flag selling lend themselves well to sponsorship. (See Chapter 6 on how to organize house-to-house and street collections.) Remember that collectors must be sixteen or over. The adult supervising the event can act as the marshal, signing the participants' sponsorship forms.

Sponsored community work: Even more virtuous than sponsored fund-raising is sponsored community work. The main problem is finding appropriate work. Some areas have volunteer bureaux which will do just that; in other areas one can contact the local Council of Social Service. If there is no such organization in your area, then contact the local hospitals, including mental hospitals, or the office of the Director of Social Services.

The participants must be carefully supervised, for not only do they have to be protected, but so do those receiving the service from them, who are often old people. Some participants are likely to need reminding that they are there to work, not to lark about; this should be done good humouredly—they are volunteers, not prisoners. Local organizations, such as Task Force, may be willing to lend any necessary equipment, such as ladders and buckets for redecorating and garden tools for gardening jobs. Providing transport may be a problem, so make sure that your marshals have cars. Organize the work to be done by two or more participants working together, as it is safer and more enjoyable.

Organize a list of the jobs or type of jobs, to be done, before the sponsored work-in, as this will reassure parents of participants and encourage sponsors. The sponsorship form when completed by the supervisor should include information on the type of work undertaken.

The local press are likely to be sympathetic to sponsored community work, so make sure that they are contacted both for prior publicity, to gain sponsors and participants, and send a press release after the event.

Collections

Children make appealing collectors, but since the law requires them to be sixteen or over they should be accompanied by an adult who does the actual collecting. Since most sixth formers are over sixteen, as are many youth club members and students, and they often enjoy house-to-house or street collecting, it is sensible to invite schools and youth clubs to help in any house-to-house or street collection held in their area. (On collecting generally see Chapter 6.)

Carol singing is particularly suitable for children. They should be accompanied by an adult, not only because of the laws restricting collections to those over sixteen, but also for their own protection on dark evenings.

There is no legal restriction on children collecting for charity from family or friends, and some charities issue cards with tear-off stamps, which can be stuck on the card in units of, say, 5p, the aim being to cover the card completely. The stamps also provide a useful way of receipting donations.

Collection of re-cyclable material Young people are often the most conscientious collectors of waste material, such as bottles and paper. The collections can be organized by the school or youth club, or by a group of children in their own immediate neighbourhood. It is useful for the charity to be able to prepare a brief introduction sheet on how to set about organizing such a collection. If organizing a collection within an area, do not forget to invite schools and youth groups to participate. (See the section on re-cycling collections, pp. 32–3.)

Other fund-raising ideas for young people

Schools or youth groups wishing to raise funds for charity can devise many ways of doing so. Below are listed some ways in which children can raise money—whether grouped into schools or youth groups or acting independently. They should not be initiated by the charity, but rather should be undertaken by the children, with the charity simply receiving the money. It is, however, appropriate for the charity to list them in a list of fund-raising ideas and to give general directions especially on publicity, on such a checklist.

Bazaars and fêtes.
Beetle drives.
Bingo.
Plays or puppet shows.
Sweet making or baking—selling the produce.
Selling used toys and comics at a stall outside the house or in the school playground.
Organizing table tennis or tennis tournaments with competitors paying to enter and spectators paying to watch.
Bob-a-job weeks.
For older children: a babysitting service in their neighbourhood, or a dog walking service, or a shopping service for busy housewives.

Social events for teenagers

In certain communities there is a tradition for charity aid committees to organize social events, such as dances, discotheques, rambles, car rallies, bridge or backgammon evenings, Guy Fawkes parties, barbecues, and for them to provide the social life for the teenagers of the community. It is at such events that youngsters meet, and in some communities it is a recognized way of finding a spouse.

It is not sensible for a charity to initiate events in such a community, but rather to try to organize an aid group to undertake the promotion of such events on its behalf. (For organizing a group, see p. 24.)

Universities and colleges

Students, whether at universities, colleges, art schools or polytechnics, can be highly efficient and strongly motivated fundraisers. Lists of universities and colleges can be found in the *Education Authorities Directory* (School Government Publishing Company).

There are many ways of approaching students for funds. Firstly, many universities and colleges hold Rag Days to raise funds for a variety of local and national charities. To become one of the recipients, contact, in the first instance, the secretary of the students' union, and find out the name of the Rag committee chairman. Contact him and ask how applications for a grant from Rag proceeds should be made. Invite him, and other Rag committee members, to visit your charity to see something of its work. Alternatively, an appeal can be sent to all universities and colleges, asking for a grant from Rag proceeds. Not all will, in fact, have Rags, and will tell you so; but nearly all do make some charity allocations. The letter should be sent in the autumn term, since most Rag committees draw up their allocations lists then.

An appeal can be sent to all students' unions, addressed to the president, for a specific campaign. It helps if the appeal is endorsed by a body such as the National Union of Students, or by some well-respected individual (it is difficult to find someone likely to appeal to all students).

If your charity has a local college or university, then try to establish links with it: inviting the union council to visit you and suggesting ways in which they could help—by house-to-house collecting, by carol singing, by acting as flag sellers, by organizing a special Rag Day if they do not already have one, or a sponsored stunt, like walking backwards. Contact parallel interest groups in colleges throughout the country. For example, a legal aid centre could contact university law societies; a medical research charity all medical students; etc. Ask them to help in specific campaigns, and perhaps do one fund-raising event a term. Try to establish your own aid group at the college. Ask the President of the union for his advice: he may know of some students likely to be enthusiastic. Hold a launching meeting, perhaps with a film or interesting speaker, and see how many people you can sign up.

The organization, Third World First, based in Oxford, collects banker's orders from students for charities. The main beneficiaries are overseas aid charities, but others can benefit, as the student can specify any charity. It is helpful to contact Third World First and make sure that your cause is known to them, and discuss the possibilities of a joint campaign (this would mean going round halls of residence or colleges, and asking the students to sign banker's order forms—in other words, a rather sophisticated type of house-to-house collecting).

Students are regarded as an important group by many charities, not just because of their fund-raising potential, but because they are expected to form an élite, whose opinions are important in determining attitudes to the charity's cause. Remember, too, that universities can be approached for expertise as well as fund-raising. Academics are generally sympathetic to requests for help, and flattered to receive them. Academics can be asked to evaluate projects, devise equipment or, in the case of business schools, even act as management consultants for the charity.

Summary

Young people, whether at school, college or university, can be enthusiastic fund-raisers. More important, the sympathy created for any charity's beneficiaries will have a long-term effect. Schools, colleges, youth clubs and universities prove an organizational framework for a charity's educational and fund-raising activities. Headteachers and teachers are the key figures in determining whether a school takes part in a campaign. It is more difficult to build up contact with youth clubs, which often are in need of funds themselves. The variety of ways in which young people can raise money is enormous. Traditionally, young people fund-raise by carol singing, organizing school fêtes and taking part in sponsored events.

Often the most effective fund-raising events are those devised and carried out by the young people themselves. University students can take part in specific fund-raising activities for a charity, or can organize their own Rag Day, distributing the proceeds to several charities.

3 Trusts

In law a charitable trust and a charity are virtually synonymous, but in general fund-raising terms there is a clear difference. A trust does not seek donations (though it can) as charities do: its income usually derives from its capital. It is bound by charity law to distribute its funds in accordance with its trust deed, and is thus generally restricted to giving grants to other charities and not, for example, for political purposes. The establishment of trusts has increased enormously since the war, and it is a recognized way for both individuals and firms to give to charity whilst securing major tax concessions and, thus, at least cost to themselves. Because of progressive taxation, it is now rare for an individual to give substantial amounts to charity, except through a trust of which he retains control (it is estimated that 10 per cent of new charities registered are of this type).

Trusts can be established for the same purpose as a charity:

1. The relief of poverty,
2. The advancement of religion,
3. The advancement of education,
4. Other purposes beneficial to the community.

They are bound, as are charities, to show that any donation they make falls within these four categories. Each trust will also be restricted by its trust deed, though this may be so vague as to allow the trustees a free hand, or so limiting that the trustees have to apply to the Charity Commissioners for an order of *cy près* to get the purpose of the trust updated.

Trusts are important for fund-raising charities because they form a body which is obliged to disburse its funds to charity. The amount which trusts give to charities exceeds £100 million a year. Since most trusts hold their assets in shares or property, their income fluctuates; but they still remain less dependent on economic vicissitudes than individual donors, which heightens their importance to recipient charities. Industrial giving can all but cease in times of economic recession, whereas trusts may have their incomes reduced, but still give.

Directory of Grant-Making Trusts

The task of charities wishing to solicit funds from trusts has been made considerably easier by the publication of the *Directory of Grant-Making Trusts* (Charities Aid Foundation of the NCSS). The *Directory* lists over 2,000 trusts in the UK, which make grants for charitable purposes. It excludes trusts with annual incomes below £500, or those whose giving is limited to an area less than a county or county borough. The *Directory* is updated annually.

Trusts are listed in alphabetical order (with full details) and also under subject heading and geographically. In the alphabetical listing information includes the name and address of the correspondent (to whom applications must be made), the trustees, the year the trust was founded, its objects and any restrictions on its giving. It also includes details of the trust's finances (although these are a bit outdated by the time of publication) and, if known, the current policy of the trustees.

The *Directory* also lists, where the information is available, some past grants made by trusts, with a rough indication of the size of the grants. This information is difficult to use effectively, as some trusts will continue to give to past recipients, others will specifically exclude them and even similar charities. It is of most use in showing the size of grants the trust may make—many inexperienced charity fund-raisers are nonplussed to receive a £5 donation from one of the richest trusts, especially if a great deal of effort has been put into tailoring an application.

Although there is little doubt that the *Directory of Grant-Making Trusts* is an absolute boon to fund-raisers, certain care should be exercised in its use. It should be noted that information is not always reliable. Despite the care of the editors, not all entries are verified by the trusts. Entries which have not been verified are indicated in the text. In some cases inaccuracies occur because the trustees of a particular trust are not as frank and honest as they might be. They allege that the trust's funds are fully committed (though this may not be the case), because they fear a flood of applications. Some may claim as 'objects of the trust' and 'policy of the trustees' policies which they do not in fact follow—perhaps not liking to admit that giving is by idiosyncrasy. In general, where trusts list under objectives 'general charitable purposes', it means that the trustees are empowered to give to anything, at their discretion. The *Directory* lists these trusts separately, with their incomes, which is some guide to the worth of applying to them on the offchance.

As a general rule, the more you know about trusts the more likely you are to succeed. The information in the *Directory* is only a guide. It is through replies to one's applications that more reliable information can be gleaned. The practice of trusts of sending duplicated refusals—'Your appeal has been considered and regretfully rejected'—is to be deplored. It would cost them no more to include information on their giving policies that would be a guide to future applicants, for example, 'Your appeal has been considered, and rejected, as the trustees are restricting donations to (a) cancer research, (b) homes for the aged, (c) local charities.'

How to find trusts not listed in the *Directory of Grant-Making Trusts*

Trusts with annual incomes under £500, and those which restrict their giving to a geographical area not greater than a county or county borough are not listed in the *Directory of Grant-Making Trusts*. Yet for many local charities, these may be the very trusts which are most likely to respond to their applications. Unfortunately, finding out about trusts which are not listed in the *Directory* can be an arduous business. All charities, whether fund-raising or grant-making, are listed in the Central Register of Charities and it is possible through judicious use of the index to find out trusts which give to specific causes, and those which give to specific geographical areas. Full copies of the Central Register of Charities are kept both at the London and Liverpool offices of the Charity Commissioners. Copies of the Register for charities operating in their areas are held by each local authority. The Charity Register includes information on the purpose of the charity, its approximate income and to whom applications should be addressed. Whilst the task of sifting through the Central Register is perfectly possible, it is tedious. There are over 100,000 registered charities, and as only one-third of them have incomes of over £100 it means that a great deal of judicious skimming is needed to find those in a position to make grants.

Giving to UK charities is not restricted to UK trusts; some foreign trusts are very generous to UK causes—think of the Gulbenkian Foundation and the Ford Foundation. Foreign based trusts which give to UK causes are, as a rule, large and give substantial grants, usually for specific purposes. American trusts are listed in *The Foundation Directory* (Foundation Center, New York). European trusts are listed in *The Guide to European Foundations* (Editor: Mrs A. Farnetti, Giovanni Agnelli Foundation, Milan), and a directory of trusts throughout the world which give on an international basis is *World Foundations* (Europa Publications).

For the charity which intends to try to secure funds from trusts year after year, it is sensible to try to build up as comprehensive a catalogue as possible of information to supplement that of the *Directory of Grant-Making Trusts* and the other directories. The replies to applications, whether rejections or acceptances, should be noted, so that future applications can be tailored accordingly.

Trustees

All trusts have trustees, who are responsible for their correct administration. It is the trustees who are entrusted to carry out the purposes as laid down in the trust deed. It is the trustees who make the decisions on which charities receive grants. In practice, the influence of one trustee may be pre-eminent. Some trustees may be mere figureheads and take little interest in the trust's activities, rarely attending meetings or concerning themselves as to its decisions; in other cases, where an individual has used his personal fortune to start a trust, that one person may appoint as fellow trustees those whom he can dominate, and so retain control over his charitable giving. The Charity Commissioners have in the past publicly rebuked those who believe that they can form a trust and yet retain control of it without public scrutiny: a charity or charitable trust cannot be private.

It is estimated that as few as thirty trusts in the UK have any full-time staff. In those that do, the clerk (as he is generally called) may have considerable influence, not only in sifting the applications but even in their eventual selection. In other cases he may be as his title suggests—merely a clerk.

It is hard for a charity when applying to a trust to know how much influence the individual trustees wield, and whether a donation depends on securing the personal interest of one of the trustees. It rarely hurts an applicant if his cause will be championed by one of the trustees, but it must be said that a few clerks resent what they regard as unfair tampering with the correct procedures, and will devote considerable energy to devising closely argued opposition to such trustee-linked applications. In other instances a trustee who knows a charity (or more usually its officers) will declare an interest and decline to champion the cause. For a majority of trusts, however, a trustee's personal recommendation of a cause is the best guarantee of success.

As a general rule, the older the trust the more objective its grant-making is likely to be, because it will not be ruled by the founder (whose co-trustees may be place-men). Trusts with large disposable incomes may be forced to recruit expert advisers who can evaluate applications, and thus move towards a more objective policy, in which the individual trustee's idiosyncrasies become less important. It is easy to give away £1,000 a year to charity on an uninformed impulse; it is harder to dispense with £100,000 in that way.

Even where trustees adopt a coherent policy on how to disburse funds, and thus reduce the practice of trustees' using trust resources to meet their own charity whims, the trustees cannot be regarded as impartial. As a body, trustees can be stigmatized as conservative, successful, wealthy; either successful businessmen or professional men. Deprived groups, who are likely to be the ultimate recipients of trust funds, are almost certainly grossly under-represented, and a trustee from a deprived background has almost certainly left it behind. These characteristics of trustees are reflected in the grant-making policies of trusts. Whilst the justification for the existence of trusts (and charities in general)—which gain at the public expense through tax concessions—is that they can undertake pioneering work and respond with greater flexibility to changing needs than can government, in fact most trusts are conservative, pioneer nothing knowingly, and have a doctrinaire belief in self-help. When applying to trusts, this should be borne in mind—the successful applicant is likely to share the values of the trustees, at least ostensibly.

How to apply to trusts

Usually applications to trusts are by writing, and there is a correspondent to whom all applications are addressed. If a trustee is personally known to a charity's officers or trustees, then an informal approach, asking how best to frame an appeal to the trust, and soliciting his influence, should be made. Where a trust has a full-time clerk, it is useful to ask him if there is an official application form, or preferred method of application. Where an application to a trust involves a great deal of preparation and gleaning of specific information, it is particularly sensible to make sure that it follows the prescribed form, and includes all requisite information.

Some trustees are clearly influenced by meeting the supplicant face-to-face. If you want to meet the correspondent, you can write and ask for an appointment so that you can discuss your planned application. If you prefer to telephone, then remember that in many cases the correspondent is a solicitor and, given the address, one can trace the telephone number by finding the firm through the Yellow Pages. Some people swear by personal approaches, but it must be remembered that it is as easy for a person to be disliked as for him to be persuasive. At least a written application is neutral.

There are two types of applications to trusts. The first are those tailor-made for a specific trust, which will contain a great deal of detail, including financial detail. The second type are general appeals, which are sent to hundreds of trusts, seeking general support. One tailor-makes appeals when the chances of success are good, and the amount involved is substantial, or when a prescribed form of application is required. A general application which is sent to several hundred trusts should be made as little like a circular as possible for a printed letter, by 'topping and tailing' each application individually, that is, writing in by hand the salutation and signature on each letter.

Any application, whether general or specific, should include:

1. Background information on the charity (except if it is too well known to need such an introduction). This may include details on when it was founded, by whom, for what purpose and what the charity has achieved since its foundation.

2. A description of either the particular project or aspect of the charity's work for which it is seeking trust funds.

3. Emphasis, where relevant, on the pioneering aspects of the work, and on its catalytic nature, through which it will have a disproportionately great effect for the resources involved.

4. Indication of the particular qualifications and suitability of those chosen to carry out the project.

5. Information on the cost of the project and on the financial position of the charity. Take care that these figures are accurate and tally with those in the charity's annual report—usually one of the trustees will take the trouble to check any figures.
6. If relevant, indication whether the project will need indefinite funding or if it is hoped that it will become self-sufficient, perhaps by securing statutory funding.
7. Indication of what support has been forthcoming from other sources, especially if this adds respectability to the application.
8. An attempt to show why the work the charity proposes to undertake, if finance is secured, is of such importance that it should be supported before the work of other applicants.

It may help an application if the letter is signed by some well-known person, or if the application is endorsed by him in some way, for example, by a covering letter. If the charity is unknown, then a big name can add weight to an appeal. On the other hand, a well-known person may lend his name to a cause, but not be prepared to top and tail several hundred letters, so the added weight of his name is counterbalanced by the application seeming like a circular rather than a personal approach. Often a suitable name can be found amongst the charity's trustees, and he should be prepared to do the necessary work to personalize the appeal. For some trusts the issue of who signs the appeal may be crucial—the rule is that if the appeal is for salaries and the running costs of the organization it should come from the trustees, not the staff.

The form of application is also important. Many trustees are busy and will not be prepared to read through a twenty-page application, so it is sensible to write a covering letter, mentioning the main points of the application, and to provide the more detailed information in a separate project proposal. It is also useful to include some printed literature on the charity's work—usually the annual report, as this will include the charity's accounts—and some trustees insist on seeing them before an application can be considered. As has been said before, care should be taken in selecting support literature: the fact that there are 5,000 spare copies of a leaflet lying round in the office does not mean that it should be sent out to trusts! The tone of the material should be appropriate—restrained rather than brash, and rather more sophisticated than a publication for a mass audience. If planning a large mailing to trusts, it might be worth considering preparing a special leaflet, which would re-emphasize the main points of the application.

If re-applying to a trust, try to vary the style of the support literature, as this will add interest to your renewed appeal. It makes sense to emphasize different aspects of the charity's work each year —for example, a research project one year, information on the charity's beneficiaries another, and impact of the charity's campaigning in the third year.

Why trusts reject applications

However well-written and planned an application to a trust, however eminent its sponsors, and worthy the cause, it does not mean the application will succeed. It would be very, very unusual for any trust to have sufficient resources to meet all requests for help, even if it wanted to. Usually, trusts either fail to reply to unsuccessful applications, or send back a formal rejection which gives little indication of the true reason for refusal.

The main reason why trusts reject appeals is that they do not have sufficient funds. Their capital may be held in property or shares, and thus their income fluctuates in accord with these markets. The 1974 fall in the stock market halved and even quartered the incomes of some trusts, and their grants had to be reduced accordingly. It is sensible for a charity which is applying to a trust to satisfy itself, as far as it can, that the trust has the resources to meet the applicant's request. This can be done by checking the income of the trust in the *Directory of Grant-Making Trusts* (although the figures are out of date by the time of publication, they act as a rough guide). Even more pertinent is the size of grants which the trust makes. Some very large trusts which give away tens of thousands of pounds a year do so in £10 grants! It is useful to glean what information there is in the *Directory* on past giving by a trust, as indication is given of the size of grant made: for example, if it was a two-, three- or four-figure number.

Many trusts, when rejecting appeals, declare their funds to be committed. This may or may not be the case. Some few trusts plan their giving on a quinquennial basis, so their income is indeed committed years in advance. Other trusts repeat grants to charity automatically, so commit their funds almost indefinitely. It is difficult for those planning a general appeal to trusts to judge whether a trust's claim that its funds are fully committed should be taken to mean a commitment for the next five years or indefinitely. After all, how do the trustees decide to re-apportion grants at the end of the current period of commitment, if not on the basis of applications received? A policy of greater frankness by trusts would save energy all round. If a charity receives specific information that a trust's income is committed, then it is not worth re-applying each year, although it might be worth re-applying in alternate years, or applying annually, sending a covering note to say that although the trust's funds may be committed at the moment your appeal is designed to keep the trustees up-to-date with the work of the charity, in the hope that when the trust has funds available for distribution it will give sympathetic consideration to the charity.

Whilst some trusts repeat grants almost automatically, others specifically will not. They like to spread their grants around, some so much that they will not even give to charities in the same field of interest as a previous recipient. Usually trusts following these policies will tell applicants. These types of policies make it hard to use the *Directory of Grant-Making Trusts'* information on past giving, since it would be natural to assume, for example, that a trust which had given a four-figure sum for housing might have a special interest in the housing field and support other charities working in this area of interest; in fact, it may exclude all charities in the housing field, having supported one.

Faced with a veritable avalanche of applications, some trusts, after discarding the most ludicrous, simply compile a list, placing new applicants at the bottom, and work down the list each year. Some will reject an appeal one year but feel reluctant to do so repeatedly, so perseverance will be rewarded.

Some trusts will consider only those appeals which are backed by well-known people. This may apply if the charity is relatively unknown, and the trustees want the stamp of respectability which a well-known figure may give. In other cases trustees seek evidence that those expert in the field are supporting an application. This does not arise very often, simply because most applications to trusts are for obviously good causes which use well-tried methods; but in cases where the application is for innovative work it will carry a great deal of weight to have the backing of leading experts, and failure to do so may lead to automatic rejection of the application.

Whilst well-known patrons add respectability to an application, a list of rich, well-known patrons on the charity's notepaper is likely to bring summary rejection from some trusts. It is felt that the charity should tap its resources first, before approaching trusts, and failure to do so reflects badly on the management of the charity. Also, it is the unestablished, unpopular charities which cannot rely on rich patrons who most need trust funds, and whose receipt of them is the best defence of the privileged position of trusts. One supplicant was advised by the administrator of one of the country's largest trusts that knowing a trustee was the best way to ensure a grant; if the supplicant had known one of the trustees, all members of one of the country's richest families, he probably would not have needed the trust's money.

It is undoubtedly, though regrettably, the case that the most usual cause for an application to a trust being accepted is that it is sponsored by one of the trustees; and it follows, therefore, that since such appeals use up most trust funds, all others are rejected because not championed by one of the trustees. To try to overcome this cause for rejection, a charity can seek to interest a trustee in its cause. Trustees are often listed in the *Directory of Grant-Making Trusts*, and the bigger trusts usually have well-known trustees. A personal approach is most generally successful if it comes from someone known to the trustee, preferably someone from his peer group. One of the charity's own trustees or patrons may often, on enquiry, be able to boast such an acquaintance. He should be well briefed on the charity's application and asked to make an informal approach to the trustee. Through such an approach it should be possible to find out how best to frame a formal application; what measure of support the trustee involved is prepared to give, and how crucial that support will be. In advising on how best to make the approach, the trustee may also suggest which aspects of the charity's work are most usefully emphasized.

Nobbling trustees is a talent: a good fund-raiser will develop a mental catalogue of those who are of proven ability in this sphere. A clumsy approach to a trustee can ruin the chance of an application, even for a period of years to come. However good the fund-raiser, he will have failures and successes, and in trying to nobble trustees these may well be spectacular.

Follow-up

When a trust makes a grant to a charity, it is only courteous to keep it informed as to the progress of the work it has supported. This does not mean that a £5 grant from a trust should involve the charity in the special preparation of progress reports, at a labour cost to the charity of £20; but where a trust has given substantially it is entitled to know how the money has been spent, and may well repeat the grant if the progress report contains an implicit request for further aid.

All trusts, as all donors, should be placed on the charity's mailing list. It is generally most useful to file them as a separate group. If the charity sends out copies of an annual report to its donors, then it is sensible to include trusts; but they should be excluded from mailings such as Christmas card catalogues. When undertaking a mass mailing to trusts, a note can be added to those which have given before, yet whose level of giving does not warrant a specific appeal, mentioning their previous generosity. However small a past donation, the donor likes to feel the charity values it.

Summary

Much of the information in this chapter on how to apply to trusts, and their reasons for rejecting appeals, must appear contradictory. Try to secure the support of a trustee—do not try to secure the support of a trustee, lest it alienate the clerk; apply to trusts which are known to have given to related fields—do not expect grants from such sources; do not waste time applying to trusts whose funds are committed—disregard claims that funds are committed. None of these statements is wrong; it is simply that some are wrong for some trusts and right for others. Accurate information on all trusts is unobtainable, so the fund-raiser has to surmise from partial information which approach is most likely to be favoured by a particular trust. The variety of likes and dislikes of trustees have been mentioned here, so that the fund-raiser can at least consider the possibilities. Trusts give over £100 million a year to UK charities, so are an important source of charitable income.

4 Industry

British industry gives an estimated £35 million to UK charities each year. This represents a lower level of company donation than prevails in the USA, but provides a substantial source of funds, of particular importance to some charities.

The greatest part of company giving is to education and research (possibly as much as two-thirds of the total value of the donations) in areas related to the company's activity. In part this is thought to be because it is easier to justify such giving to the shareholders, as being in the company's interest, but mainly the reason is traditional. Company giving to education is usually confined to higher education or public schools—in the attempt to raise the standard of management recruits; virtually nothing is given to raise the level of factory workers' education, which would arguably be of greater benefit to the firm and its shareholders.

Industry has come to regard itself as stepping into the role of rich patron, which has been vacated by individuals since the imposition of high taxation. In fact firms give away shareholders' money and, although unlikely to be found at fault in law, reluctance to be challenged by the shareholders on this, as any other issue, tends to make a firm's charitable giving rather conservative, and perhaps limit its scale. (Interestingly, shareholders have shown themselves very unconcerned about charitable contributions, although since 1967 companies have had to declare the level of charitable giving along with their donations to political parties.)

Although *en masse* industry donates considerable amounts to charity, the level of donations made by individual firms is surprisingly small. Of the top 100 industrial givers listed by the Wells

Group, that listed fiftieth gave £50,000 to charity in 1973, the hundredth largest gave £18,256. Only one company, and that is the Wellcome Foundation, which is a special case, regularly gives over £1 million a year to charity. (Several companies give over £1 million if their donations to specialized technical training or research, which are held by the Inland Revenue to be in 'furtherance of trade' and therefore tax deductible, are included.) So although British companies may not be the source of such largesse as is sometimes imagined, it is still true that industry, along with trusts, provides a potential source of larger-scale donations than are normally available from individuals.

How firms give

Since donations to charity are not tax deductible expenses, companies can choose to give to charity through straight, one-off donations, through covenants (allowing the charity to recover the tax), through taking advertising space in the charity's brochures, through gifts in kind either for resale by the charity or for its use and, lastly, through joint promotions and sponsorship.

1. *Straight donations*

A company may commit no specific amount to charitable giving, but rather deal with charity appeals on an ad hoc basis, varying the amount given with the urgency of the appeals. This practice is clearly more common amongst small firms than amongst large ones.

Other companies work within a general charity budget, and may increase or decrease the amount available according to profits. Some may give one-off donations to a variety of causes; others will regard a donation as an annual commitment and act accordingly. It is very difficult for a charity to know how each firm will act, and so donations from industry (unless the management are well known to the charity's managers) should not be depended upon: because a firm gave once is no guarantee that it will do so again, especially if its giving is related to business profitability.

2. *Covenanted giving*

A firm which signs a covenant benefiting a charity enables the charity not only to recover the corporation tax (thus raising the level of the donation) but also to plan its activities with an assured income. As with individuals signing covenants, many firms show themselves reluctant to undertake the commitment of a covenant.

Many firms however sign discretionary covenants with the Charities Aid Foundation. Although the company is committed to a certain level of charitable giving (it may be a percentage of profits or a fixed amount), the recipients can be changed at the direction of the company, so that it can give to a hundred different charities a year, if it so chooses. Considering that this raises the company's charitable budget at no cost to itself (through the tax refund), it is surprising and regrettable that more companies do not use the scheme.

A company which gives through covenants, either directly to the charity or through the Charities Aid Foundation, is unlikely to cut back its charity budget at the first hint of economic adversity (though some may link their covenants to profit levels). This should be remembered, as many charities seem reluctant to approach industry when times seem bad, in the mistaken belief that companies cease to donate to charity when profits fall: companies may want to, but are forced to maintain their covenant commitments.

Some companies give through charitable trusts, whose fortunes may or may not be tied up with those of the firm—for example, the assets of the trust may be a company's shares. Where a company has a trust, it usually signifies a generous commitment to charity and a set of rules governing the dispersal of funds, as opposed to general company giving, which is usually of a random, idiosyncratic nature.

3. *Advertising space*

The charity brochure is the main money-spinner for most charity functions (see Chapter 7). Many companies have special budgets for such charity advertising, and prefer to donate to charity in this way, since not only are they doing good, but are seen to be doing good. What firms expect to pay for advertising in charity publications varies, but a full-page advertisement in a ball or film premiere brochure is on average about £100, while covers and colour pages are charged at a higher rate and part pages are proportionately lower. When asking a firm to advertise, be sure to stipulate page size and method of printing, whether offset litho (requiring artwork) or conventional letterpress printing (needing a block).

4. *Gifts in kind*

Many firms will give some of their products to charity for resale or use in the charity's work. Tombola gifts, raffle prizes, new stock for a charity's gift shops, are all given. It is a question of building up good records of which companies give what, so that the search for gifts becomes less onerous the second time round.

A circular letter asking for gifts for resale can be usefully sent to large retail groups, or mail order companies, which may have left-over stock they are happy to clear. For gifts for a tombola or raffle, a large-scale mailing is not cost effective, and personal approaches to local stores usually yield the best results.

Apart from gifts for resale, firms are often generous in donating goods and services for use to the charity in its work. For example, toy manufacturers may give toys to homes for handicapped children, or food manufacturers may give gifts of jams or biscuits to old people's homes. Appeals for gifts of this kind are most successful where the company is in the neighbourhood of the charity concerned. Some firms will respond to appeals for goods or services which facilitate the charity's work, for example gifts of paper or envelopes or typewriters, or will offer clerical assistance with large mailings.

5. *Joint promotions and sponsorship*

A fairly recent development in industrial support for charity has been the growth of joint promotions, whereby the company promotes its goods by associating them with the charity's cause. In some cases the charity gives a 'seal of approval' to the goods, the company paying a royalty to the charity. This method is open to criticism, as the charity must satisfy itself of the absolute desirability and worth of the item endorsed, and can damage its good name by associating itself with unsatisfactory goods (and even when, objectively, the goods are satisfactory, some consumer is bound to be dissatisfied). A charity has to be more jealous of its reputation than a company, since it depends on goodwill for its survival.

More usual than this straightforward endorsement is the type of joint promotion whereby the firm gives a specific donation for charity in return for tokens sent in by the consumer. Each token may be worth 2p or 10p, and the total amount to be donated to the charity usually has a fixed upper limit. The profits to charity can be considerable: in 1973 the World Wildlife Fund claimed that joint promotions brought in revenue 'in excess of six figures per annum'. The profits to the company can be similarly gratifying: in 1972 Kiwi Guard Polish stimulated sales over 25 per cent during a campaign in conjunction with the Spastics Society—the charity's profit was £1,000.

Charities involved in joint promotions put a high value on the publicity gained by such exercises, since the charity's name is brought before thousands, even millions, of people. But it should be recognized that not all members of the public like such schemes, and some feel that the charity is selling itself cheap, for quick gain. The economics of these joint promotions can seem a bit silly to consumers—2p given for each returned token, when postage is more than three times that amount—but they can be very successful.

Not all charities are likely to be invited to participate in joint promotions. Those with a popular image—children, animals and the environment—seem the favoured groups. A charity is usually approached by a manufacturer or advertising agency, which proposes the joint promotion; it is not usual or generally effective for the charity to seek out the manufacturer to promote such schemes.

Sponsorship by companies, usually of sporting, though sometimes of cultural, events has increased over the last decade to an estimated £10 million a year. The biggest spenders are the tobacco companies, anxious to associate their products with clean, manly sports. Sponsorship is simply a prestige exercise for the company involved—it brings the name of the product before the public in a favourable context. But companies are beginning to question the value of sponsorship, and there is some evidence that the funds available for sponsorship are declining. But there is nothing to stop a charity wishing to promote an event, such as a series of concerts or football matches, trying to find a company to sponsor the event. Such approaches are most likely to succeed where one of the company's directors is interested in the activity concerned.

Why firms give

Not all firms have a well-defined policy on charity giving, and often where rules do exist they are disregarded, or used only as an excuse for not giving. As would seem likely, those firms which give most are the most likely to work out some coherent policy—though it may be no more sophisticated than limiting all donations to £10 or giving only to charities supported by the managing director's wife. Firms complain bitterly about the number of appeals they have to deal with, and many form charity allocations committees to deal with appeals, so that the managing director has time to deal with the running of the firm.

One can distinguish six main reasons why firms will support a charity, and which they use to justify both giving at all and their choice of charity.

1. *Creating goodwill*

Firms like to be seen to be 'good citizens'. A company will often tie its level of donations to that of similar companies, not liking to be thought less generous than its peers. Creating goodwill is an especially strong motive in industrial support for local charities. Interestingly, although firms give the majority of their donations to local causes, the actual amount given to such charities is less than one-quarter of industry's charitable giving.

2. *Support of allied causes*

It helps the company's image to be associated with certain causes. For example, the pet food manufacturers want to be identified with animal charities, thus implying that their production of pet food is based on love of animals rather than merely love of profit. In some cases the company's attempt to associate with the cause is rather dubious—like tobacco firms and cancer research—but generally the links are obvious to both donor and recipient.

These two reasons can be termed image building. Companies may like to publicize such giving—for example, through advertising in the charity's publications or being listed as a patron.

3. *Obliging particular customers*

If a business customer asks for support for a particular cause, there has to be a good reason to refuse his appeal, although the amount given may be considerably less than that asked for. If the firm has a charity allocations committee and a defined charitable policy, it is easier to refuse such requests, but many, if not most, firms give on an ad hoc basis, and so are particularly open to requests from customers and business colleagues. Most of this giving is on a knock-for-knock basis: the directors of the charity will solicit help for their pet charities or those of their wives, from their suppliers.

Table 1 *The 100 largest giving companies in the UK*

Rank	Name	Charitable giving 1973
1.	Wellcome Foundation (wholly owned by Wellcome Trust)	£2,642,334
2.	Distillers	£2,110,000 (includes £2,030,000 for Thalidomide children)
3.	ICI	£471,000
4.	Shell Petroleum	£331,000
5.	Unilever	£284,000
6.	Marks & Spencer	£280,000
7.	British Petroleum	£262,865
8.	Barclays Group	£215,108
9.	National Westminster Bank	£193,622
10.	IBM	£172,000
11.	Imperial Group	£150,252
12.	Midland Bank	£132,000
13.	Rank Organization	£115,398
14.	Courtaulds	£111,172
15.	Lloyds Bank	£100,031
16.	Ford Motor	£93,000
17.	Esso Petroleum	£88,781
18.	BAT Group	£86,678
19.	J. Sainsbury	£86,000
20.	Dunlop Holdings	£86,000
21.	Kodak	£85,000
22.	S. Pearson & Son	£82,160
23.	John Lewis	£82,000
24.	Guinness	£80,449
25.	GKN	£80,313
26.	Philips Electrical	£80,086
27.	F. W. Woolworth	£79,000
28.	Tube Investments	£77,000
29.	General Electric	£71,000
30.	Joseph Lucas	£70,700
31.	Associated Portland	£69,266
32.	Rank Hovis McDougall	£68,000
33.	Bank of England	£63,300
34.	Whitbread	£60,473
35.	Gallagher	£59,526

Table 1 *cont.*

Rank	Name	Charitable giving 1973
36.	Allied Breweries	£58,251
37.	Commercial Union	£57,445
38.	Beecham Group	£57,000
39.	Cadbury Schweppes	£55,000
40.	Reed International	£55,000
41.	Prudential Association	£54,686
42.	National Commercial Bank	£54,000
43.	P & O Steamship	£53,672
44.	Hawker Siddeley	£53,000
45.	Turner & Newall	£52,394
46.	Metal Box	£52,000
47.	Rio Tinto Zinc	£52,000
48.	Slater Walker	£50,735
49.	UDS Group	£50,472
50.	Boots	£50,000
51.	Burmah Oil	£50,000
52.	Glaxo Holdings	£48,000
53.	Smith & Nephew	£47,000
54.	Pilkington Bros	£46,000
55.	Carrington Viyella	£45,000
56.	British Leyland	£43,000
57.	Rothmans International	£41,342
58.	General Accident	£39,000
59.	Charter Consolidated	£38,095
60.	International Computers	£38,000
61.	Tate & Lyle	£36,515
62.	Bass Charrington	£33,539
63.	Debenhams	£33,536
64.	British Home Stores	£33,000
65.	British Oxygen	£32,000
66.	Thomas Tilling	£32,000
67.	W. H. Smith	£31,000
68.	Hill Samuel Group	£31,000
69.	Massey Ferguson	£30,795
70.	Trust Houses Forte	£30,300
71.	Rowntree Mackintosh	£30,000
72.	H. J. Heinz	£28,611
73.	The Plessey Co.	£28,530

Table 1 *cont.*

Rank	Name	Charitable giving 1973
74.	C. T. Bowring	£28,206
75.	Tootal	£28,000
76.	Royal Insurance	£27,000
77.	International Nickel	£26,840
78.	Coats Patons	£26,813
79.	British Commonwealth Shipping	£26,728
80.	Schroders	£26,000
81.	Sears Holdings	£26,000
82.	Legal & General	£25,832
83.	Bank of Scotland	£25,665
84.	Reckitt & Colman	£25,000
85.	Spillers	£24,337
86.	Fisons	£23,065
87.	Pearl Assurance	£22,872
88.	Sun Alliance	£22,676
89.	EMI	£22,600
90.	British Aircraft	£22,527
91.	Bowater Corporation	£22,000
92.	Norwich Union	£22,000
93.	Vickers	£21,905
94.	Scottish & Newcastle Breweries	£20,000
95.	Great Universal Stores	£20,000
96.	Associated British Foods	£20,000
97.	Chrysler UK	£19,553
98.	J. Lyons & Co.	£19,000
99.	Burton Group	£18,814
100.	Procter & Gamble	£18,256

(Figures from the Wells Collection issued by the Wells Group, 1975)

4. *Director's special interest*

In some cases the directors or founder of a company have some cause with which they are associated, and will use a substantial part of the company's charity budget in support of that cause. A director's special interest as a reason for giving can mean that the company is well informed on the charity, and can thus be argued to be giving with more discrimination than is usual; but regrettably in many cases it means that the director of a company uses shareholders' money to fulfil his personal charity obligations.

5. *Tradition*

Some companies will give to the same charities year after year, never reviewing their policy, believing themselves to enjoy a traditional relationship with the cause concerned. Since circumstances change, and especially the relative fortunes of charities, it is difficult to justify such traditional giving, except where there are other reasons for such support. A charity which finds that a company is donating to it year after year should tactfully suggest that a covenant be signed.

6. *Persistence*

Many firms do not like to keep refusing appeals from well-known charities (their compunction does not extend to repeated refusals of the less attractive causes, like unmarried mothers or the rehabilitation of drug addicts). Firms may refuse appeals for two years and donate in the third year. Unless the charity has evidence that its cause is outside the scope of the company's charitable giving, it is sensible to keep trying for a donation.

How to apply to firms

1. *Which companies to approach*

Before a charity approaches firms, it must consider what sort of charity it is, with what image, and to whom it is likely to prove attractive. Awareness of its own image will help a charity choose the firms it may successfully approach.

If the charity is of general appeal—for example, a national charity for children—then an appeal to leading firms is appropriate. Local charities should restrict their appeal to local industries, although charities should, as a rule, also approach firms in allied fields. For example, housing aid centres could approach building firms and estate agents.

Useful directories exist, listing firms, with addresses, names of managing director and chairman, and other details, such as what the firm does and its profits and capital assets. The most useful of these directories is *The Times 1,000*, which is published annually and obtainable from Times Newspapers Ltd, New Printing House Square, Gray's Inn Road, London WC1. Apart from the list of the top 1,000 firms in the UK, it also lists building societies, banks and insurance companies. If the charity wishes to extend its appeal to industry beyond the top 1,000 firms, other useful directories are *The Kompass Register of British Industry and Commerce* (Kompass), which lists member firms of the CBI (available in two volumes, or seven regional sections), and the *Guide to Key British Enterprises: a selection of prominent firms and companies in the UK engaged in primary manufacturing or distributive trades* (Dun & Bradstreet). The *Stock Exchange Official Year Book* (T. Skinner) lists companies quoted on the London Stock Exchange.

Such directories should be used selectively. It is most useful for the charity to build up a card index of firms to approach, basing the initial approach on locality or field of allied interest. Additional information on a firm's charitable giving policy can be added as it becomes available. Although building up a card index is an onerous task, maintaining it in order is quite simple, and makes subsequent appeals much easier.

Local companies can be found through a combination of *The Times 1,000*, the appropriate regional section of *The Kompass Register of British Industry and Commerce* and lists of local firms from the local Chamber of Commerce. The local Yellow Pages will also list local firms and, coupled with local knowledge, can provide a useful supplement to other sources.

If one is seeking gifts in kind, the CBI will provide lists of its member manufacturers of certain goods—for example, toys or filing cabinets. Where there is a trade association, it will usually be able to provide lists of member firms. If one is seeking advertising in a charity brochure, then, as well as firms in related fields, approaches can usefully be made to retail groups and manufacturers of consumer goods, whose products make them household names.

2. *The appeal itself*

A personal approach to the managing director or chairman of a y by a friend or acquaintance may be the most successful; s not always possible. Trustees, committee members and the charity should be asked if they have any personal con- h companies, and whether they would be prepared to make an approach. (More people will claim good contacts than actually prove to have them, so treat claims with caution.) Some charities draw their active supporters from business circles, and so can use a great deal of 'peer group' asking. Other charities simply do not enjoy this type of support. No charity should believe that this is how appeals to industry should be done, and that any other attempts must fail.

If a charity cannot organize a personal approach to the company, then a letter seeking support can be sent. The charity which is relatively unknown should either persuade a well-known individual to send the letter out in his name, or make sure it is sent out on paper naming the trustees, if they are well-known. The unknown charity must first and foremost establish its credentials, if its cause is to be even considered. A well-known national charity can send its appeals out in the name of one of its staff, although in some circumstances an approach backed by 'a name' is likely to be more effective.

The letter itself should be straightforward. It should cover the following points (not necessarily in this order):

(a) what the charity does: whom it helps and how it helps them;

(b) why the charity needs to exist: what gap its work is fulfilling;

(c) why the charity needs funds and how donations would be spent;

(d) why the cause is urgent: by implication, why support should be given for that cause rather than any other charity which approaches the firm;

(e) why the particular firm should give: for example, if the firm is local, then stress its obligation to aid local charities; if the firm makes profits from overseas trading, then emphasize the appropriateness of its help to overseas aid charities; (If the charity is sending a printed letter to hundreds of firms, it will not be able to make much of a case for a charity's appropriateness for individual firms.)

(f) if the firm's generosity is to be publicized, for example, in advertising, then make a point of the goodwill which will accrue to the company.

As in all large mailings, it is sensible to top and tail letters individually, to avoid the appearance of a circular. In some cases, as with appeals to trusts, it may be worth preparing a special appeal for a specific project, to an individual firm. Before spending days on drafting any such application, try to ascertain whether the company is likely to be sympathetic—has it supported your cause or similar ones in the past, or does it work in related fields? Also, find out if the company gives substantial amounts to charity—this can be done by checking its rank in the list of the top 100 business donors (see Table 1).

Apart from the appeal letter, some sort of support literature will be needed. The most usual choice is the charity's annual report, which will include its accounts and some general information on its work. Not all charities have an annual report—and not all those that do should consider them appropriate support literature. Support literature should not be chosen because 10,000 spare copies happen to be lying round the office. Apart from a specially produced leaflet, tailor-made for an appeal, a report undertaken by a charity on an aspect of its work, or a review of its project work might both be suitable. Try to vary the type of support literature from year to year, so that the recipient can see many aspects of the charity's work, and also so that he will not be bored by the appeal. Many firms (and trusts) will keep a charity's literature on file, and will refer to past appeals when considering a new one: this makes a variety of support literature seem even more impressive. Together with the appeal letter, the support literature should convey not only the significance of the charity's work, but also its style.

3. *The company's reply*

Not all firms asked for a donation will bother to reply. Most of those which bother to do so use a standard letter, which usually states that the firm has already made its charity allocation for the year and regrets it is unable to make a donation. This is in most cases a polite way of saying no; the charity receiving such a reply should not feel that it sent in its request for help too late in the year. Some firms go to great trouble to set out their reasons for a refusal, with a special letter from one of the directors—considering the cost of the director's time and that of the secretary who types the letter, it would make more sense if such companies sent out token donations of, say, 50p with a duplicated note.

The charity should look carefully at all refusals, and eliminate from further appeals those companies which give definite indications that any subsequent appeal will be rejected. For example, a company may state that it limits its donations to local and trade-related charities, or may confine its giving to the handicapped. In some cases such reasons are mere excuses, and if full details were given of the company's donations to charity it would be shown to bear no adherence to the company's alleged policy on charitable giving. A charity with some money to spare can keep sending appeals to companies which seem unlikely to give, and take a chance that the company was dissembling when giving its reasons for rejecting an appeal, and that it will respond to repeated requests for help. But generally, with the increased costs of postage, it is sensible for a charity to try to pare down its mailing lists to those companies which are most likely to respond.

4. *The letter of thanks*

All donations should be acknowledged, and the donor thanked, whether a firm or any other body. If the donation is particularly generous, then it is polite—and judicious—to send a follow-up report to the company, saying how the money was spent, and with what good effect. Of course, the charity hope to elicit further funds; but an appeal can be sent separately at a later date, if necessary. Even a £5 donation from a £1 million company warrants a thank-you letter—although in the circumstances it is better to refer to a 'kind donation' rather than a 'generous donation', lest one be considered sarcastic.

Summary

Industry gives an estimated £35 million to UK charities each year. Donations may be made in the form of covenants, cash donations or gifts-in-kind. They may be made by advertising in a charity's souvenir brochures, or by sponsoring its events. A company may use a charity's name in a joint promotion, aimed to boost sales, in return for which the charity receives a donation related to the success of the effort.

Companies give to charity for many reasons, not all well considered. The reasons may be summarized as: creating goodwill; image building; obliging customers; a director's special interest;

tradition; and the charity's persistence. Appeals may be sent to national or local firms and to those working in related fields. All donations should be acknowledged—however apparently miserly.

5 Covenants and legacies

Covenants

A covenant is a legal undertaking by a donor to give a specified amount to a charity, usually by seven annual payments, although the period may be longer. The tax which has already been paid by the donor can be subsequently reclaimed by the charity. It is a fairly complex way of giving, often dauntingly so, and to recover the tax a charity must comply with stringent regulations—for whilst the Inland Revenue is helpful to charities, it is not indulgent!

There are clear advantages to a charity in securing covenanted donations. First, just like hire purchase, it enables the donor to pay his donation by instalments and, hopefully, this means a larger total donation. Second, because covenant payments are made for a period greater than six years, it enables the charity to depend on the income and plan its expenditure accordingly. Third, the donation is increased, through the recovery of tax, at no expense to the donor: this concession to charities is estimated currently as worth £20 million a year to charities, though some estimates put it as high as £50 million.

To qualify for tax recovery, a charity must be accepted as qualifying for the right to benefit under Section 360 of the Taxes Act, 1970. Requests for registration should be made on Form R68 to the relevant Inspector of Taxes. The basic rules on covenants must be adhered to if the charity is not to forego its right to tax refund.

A covenant can be made by an individual or a corporate body, though the covenants of the latter must bear the corporation's seal, and in the case of partnerships all partners must sign the deed. The donor must receive no benefit from his donation, so the charity must not allow a covenantor to pay for goods or services by his covenant. The covenant must run for a period exceeding six years (usually seven annual payments) and must not be made retrospectively—that is, the first payment must be made after the date on which the covenant is signed.

There are two different types of covenants—'net form of wording' and 'gross form of wording'. In the first, most usual type, the covenantor gives a specific amount to the charity each year, and the charity recovers the tax on that amount. Thus the actual amount received by the charity varies if the basic rate of tax changes. The advantage to the charity of the net form of wording is that it is simpler to explain to the donor; the disadvantage is that the charity suffers if the income tax rate falls (but it could equally well benefit from a rise in tax levels). In the gross form of wording, the covenantor gives a sum of money which will, with the tax refund, bring the value of the covenant up to a specified amount. It is a more complex type of covenant, the amount to be paid by the covenantor being variable if tax rates vary. The advantage to the charity is that its income remains constant, though the tax rate may fluctuate. But it is difficult enough to explain covenanted giving to prospective donors without devising complications, such as possible fluctuations in the amounts due each year. For this reason, few charities encourage donors to covenant under a gross form of wording.

It is usual for charities to include a banker's order form with the covenant form, to facilitate the administration of the covenant. The charity does not have to trouble the donor each year as a covenant payment falls due, and send the many reminders that would almost certainly be necessary. It is usual to ask the covenantor to send the completed banker's order form, together with the deed of covenant, to the charity, rather than sending it straight to the bank. This enables the charity to check that it is correctly filled in, and to note which bank should make the payment, since banks have been known to forget to pay banker's orders!

Covenants cannot be varied. If they run out, and the covenantor wishes to continue payment, the covenant cannot simply be extended: a new covenant must be signed. The amount paid under covenant cannot be varied. If the donor increases the amount, the charity, though duly grateful, must treat the excess as an uncovenanted donation, for the Inland Revenue will not refund tax on the additional sum. If the covenantor decreases the amount

Sample covenant form (net form of wording):

(CHARITY'S NAME)

DEED OF COVENANT

I. . . . .

of. . . . .

hereby covenant with . . . .

. . . . .of . . . .

(hereinafter called the Charity) that for a period of. . . . . . years from the date hereof (or during the remainder of my life, whichever period shall be the shorter) I will pay to the Charity on the. . . . . .day of. . . . .(month) such a sum as after the deduction of income tax will amount to £. . . . .

Signed, sealed and delivered

Signature. . . . .

Date. . . . .

in the presence of:. . . . .

Signature of witness. . . . .

Address of witness . . . .

— —

BANKER'S ORDER

To. . . . .

(Name of bank)

. . . .

(address)

Please pay the sum of £. . . . . . . .on the. . . . . .day of. . . . . ,

19 , to . . . .

(charity's name and address)

and thereafter make like payments on the same date for. . . . years, making a total of. . . . . . . payments.

Account No. . . . . Name and address of donor

. . . .

Signature. . . . . Date . . . .

paid, the Inland Revenue will treat the lower amount as the consistent amount of the covenant, and might ask for a tax refund on the higher levels of previous payments. Except where a donor has covenanted a fixed proportion of his income, or index-linked it (in which case the Inland Revenue will allow tax to be recovered on varying amounts) the Inland Revenue will take the smallest payment as the true level of the covenant, on which tax is recoverable.

Legally, a covenant is a binding contract and cannot be broken. If a covenant form does not include a waiver in the event of a covenantor's death, then his executors are bound by the covenant. In practice it is extremely unlikely that a charity would take legal action against a defaulting covenantor. If it did, not only would his goodwill be lost, but there would be adverse publicity. Furthermore, the legal costs would make the proceedings unlikely to be profitable. Several charities include in their general leaflets on covenants a clear statement to the effect that a covenant can be ended if the covenantor falls on hard times. This attempts to allay the fears of prospective donors who might worry about committing themselves to a series of payments they might not be able to make. (In fact, inflation means that people generally feel better able to make payments in future years as their income rises.) If a covenant is broken, it is unusual for the Inland Revenue to ask for a repayment of tax refunds which have already been made on the covenant —but they could.

A charity can recover from the Inland Revenue the tax which has been paid on the donation at the standard rate—not at higher rates. If a covenantor is not liable to income tax (because of low income or non-residence), then no recovery of tax is possible. Some charities dissuade non-tax-payers from making covenants, but this seems unwise, since a dependable income is of great value to the charity.

Administering covenants

It is usual for one person in a charity to assume responsibility for administering covenants. The first task is to check each new covenant to see that it has been correctly filled in—the most obvious points to look for are that the date of the payment is on or after the date of the covenant, that all alterations are initialled by the donor and that the covenant is witnessed (in Scotland two witnesses are necessary) and where applicable that the corporation seal is affixed.

The repayment of tax must be claimed by the charity within six years of the significant financial year. The procedure varies for covenants of £30 a year or less and those over £30.

(a) Covenants over £30: The donor's signature is needed on Form R185(AP), copies of which are available from the local Inspector of Taxes. The charity should fill in the sections headed 'Annual payments under deed of covenant dated . . .' (with the date the covenant was signed); 'Gross amount of the payment from which I have deducted the tax' (with the gross annual value of the covenant); 'Amount of tax deducted by me' (with the amount of tax claimed for refund); 'Date on which payment is made' (with the date on which payment is due); and 'Consecutive number of payment' (showing if the payment is the first, second, third, etc., of the total number of payments). Also complete at the top the section, 'I certify that on paying to . . .' (with the name and address of the charity). The form should then be sent to the donor, who should complete the section 'Signature and business address and date'.

(b) Covenants of £30 or under (net value): Forms R185(AP) are needed only for the first payment of a covenant of £30 or less. This dispensation is granted on condition that the charity presents information on these covenants in a manner convenient to the Inland Revenue. For this purpose the Inland Revenue supplies Forms R248A and R248A (Summary), which simplifies the charity's procedure. (It is not obligatory to use these forms: a charity can use a form of its own devising, if it has the permission of the Chief Inspector of Taxes (Claims).)

(c) To make the claim for tax refund: When the charity has completed either Forms R185(AP) or, in the case of covenants not exceeding £30, R248A and R248A (Summary), then Form 235A should be completed and sent to the appropriate Chief Inspector of Taxes, with the original deeds of covenant (for covenants on which tax is being claimed for the first time) and Forms 185(AP) for covenants above £30. A copy of the charity's latest annual accounts should accompany the claim.

Transitional relief: Because the tax rate was lowered to 30 per cent in 1973 and charities would consequently suffer a loss of revenue due to the drop in refundable tax on covenants, the government introduced a period of transitional relief. The charity can reclaim tax at a rate higher than the basic 35 per cent on covenants entered into before 6 March 1973. The rate varies. Claims for transitional relief should be made on Form CAY/TRC5, obtainable from the office of the Chief Inspector of Taxes. The claim should be made separately from the repayment of income tax claim on covenants, and must be made within two years of the tax period concerned.

Loan covenants

Charities can try to increase their income by turning large donations into what are called loan covenants, thus enabling them to claim a tax refund on the donation. Two separate transactions are needed. First, a deed of covenant must be signed. The total donation is divided into seven equal parts and these are the amounts to be paid annually. The covenant should be for a seven-year term (the shortest possible). The second part of the loan covenant procedure is an exchange of payments. The charity receives the whole of the donation, now regarded as a loan, and pays one-seventh of it back to the donor, who then pays an equal sum back to the charity as the first instalment of his covenant. This is most simply done by arranging banker's orders for exchange of payments—the one from the charity to the donor to precede that of the donor to the charity. (The charity should ask the donor for a letter of waiver —in case of the donor's death during the operation of the covenant, which would otherwise leave the charity to pay to his heirs the sum outstanding on the loan.) It is not enough for the charity to make a book-keeping entry showing that, for example, £10 was paid to the donor on 2 April and returned to the charity on 3 April. There must, for the loan covenant to be legal, be an actual transfer of funds.

It would be to the advantage of a charity to convert donations to loan covenants, were this possible, since the tax refund brings a 35 per cent increase in the level of donation (at current rates of standard income tax). But because of legal niceties, a charity cannot write to a donor and ask him to convert his donation into a loan covenant after receiving his donation. A covenant signed after a donation has been made would be invalid, and the charity would not be able to claim tax refund on it. Nor could the charity refund the donation, and ask the donor to sign a covenant before returning his donation — because a charity would be in breach of trust if it refunded donations, except in exceptional circumstances.

The administration of loan covenants, apart from the annual exchange of funds, follows the same rules as those for other covenants.

Help in administering covenants

The Charities Aid Foundation (48 Pembury Road, Tonbridge, Kent) will undertake the administration of a charity's covenants, reclaiming tax and making sure that annual payments are made, etc., for a small fee per covenant so administered. This is a service which is of use to charities which do not wish to establish the necessary administration within their own organization.

Securing covenants

Covenants are much more difficult to secure than a single donation, because they involve a commitment over a minimum of seven years (and donors are often nervous of making any long-term financial commitments), they are a sophisticated form of giving which is not readily understood by all donors and, third, they require a long-term commitment to a specific charity, and some donors may not wish to repeat their donations but rather want to give to different charities each year.

Donors must be made aware of the possibility of covenanting donations, including loan covenants, and large charities (that is ones in which not all the donors are individually known to the charity's organizers) should include information on covenants on all appropriate literature. For example, receipts could be sent out with a leaflet on the general work of the charity, with a simple explanation of what covenants are and a covenant form on the reverse. All appeal letters should include information on covenants and a covenant form. Similarly, the charity's officials should emphasize the desirability of covenanting when speaking about the charity's work. Not all donors will respond by signing covenants, but some will, and the value to the charity, both through the tax refund and the long-term commitment, makes covenants a priority.

For one-off appeals, especially those with a small constituency, where there is a specific target to be reached, there should be an attempt to raise the bulk of the money from covenants. If a village church needs restoring and the villagers are expected to contribute the large part of the funds, then it reduces the burden on them if they can be persuaded to covenant (because tax refunds increase the donations substantially and also spread the load over many years). Similarly, if a PTA wishes to build a science wing or set up a library fund, because the donors are known to the fund-raiser they can become suitable convenantors, for the scheme can be fully explained to them and their fears assuaged. For many groups which raise funds from a virtual membership, such as a religious group, it is easier to secure covenants every seven years, with occasional boosts to the funds from functions, rather than have the bother of seemingly endless jumble sales, bingo evenings and whist drives. In such circumstances, where people are committed to the charity, they would often rather sign a covenant and avoid the pestering that a series of small-scale fund-raising events would involve them in.

Membership of organizations, such as the Ramblers' Association or a local synagogue, can be paid for by covenant. To comply with Inland Revenue rules, the donor should not receive any direct benefit.

Legacies

Like covenants, legacies are more difficult to secure than straight donations. But legacies are very important to charities—especially the older ones—and may contribute as much as half of their incomes. Indeed, the RSPCA derives 70 per cent of its income from legacies—no wonder its advertisements appealing for legacies start, 'Old ladies leaving all their money to a cats' home is no joke to us!' An estimated half to two-thirds of the population make wills, and it is through these wills that money is left to the charity. The number of legacies is increasing, but the value of the individual legacies is falling—doubtless the effect of increased taxation.

People do not like to be reminded of the certainty of their own approaching death, so appeals for legacies have to be handled carefully. There is a three-pronged strategy for securing legacies. First, existing donors must be made aware of the possibility of making a bequest to a specific charity. This is done in the same way as covenants—including information and a legacy form on general literature and having staff mention the possibilities of making legacies whenever appropriate. It is especially important to keep existing donors informed of procedures for bequeathing, as they are the most likely source of legacies. Second, a charity can advertise in the legal journals. This is done on the assumption that many people seek their solicitor's advice in drawing up their wills, and might ask, for example, for the name of a children's charity or a home for incurables or a cancer research charity; theoretically, the solicitor then turns to the *Law Society's Gazette* Appeals Issue or the *Charities Digest* and finds an appropriate registered charity. One cannot tell how often this situation in fact arises. Third, the charity devises a snappy slogan to ask for legacies, usually a pun, to lighten the whole subject, for example, 'It's a matter of life and death', (World Wildlife Fund), 'Fight cancer with a will' (Imperial Cancer Research Fund) and other frequently used slogans—'Will to live', and 'Where there's a will there's a way'. The slogans are designed to catch the eye, and make people aware of the possibility of donating posthumously.

Advertising for legacies

(See also Chapter 11.)

As with all expenditure of funds, a charity should be cautious about undertaking an advertising campaign which specifically appeals for legacies. The first question to be asked is, 'Will the cause appeal to the older members of the community?' After all, they are the people who make wills. Second, 'Will it appeal to the more prosperous amongst the elderly—what might loosely be described as the upper middle class and above—for they have the most to leave?' A charity like Release would not be wise to launch a legacy campaign, whereas charities that help old people or combat feared diseases, such as cancer, or help animals, do sustain large-scale advertising campaigns devoted to appeals for legacies. And in their advertising they often emphasize the aspects of their work calculated to appeal to slightly outmoded virtues of a generation ago. For example, an appeal for legacies on behalf of old people of gentle birth refers to the pride of old people who might not like to accept the charity of the state (!)

If convinced that your charity would appeal to wealthy middle-aged and elderly people, it is worth considering launching an advertising campaign to secure legacies—if you have the resources for a sustained campaign, for, like all advertising, it must be maintained over a period of time to achieve results. It is unlikely that your total advertising should be devoted to a legacy campaign.

Not all charities which receive a substantial part of their income from legacies do, in fact, advertise. A legator usually gives to a charity he has known about for many years, often one he was taught to venerate in childhood, so legacy giving lags behind the active period in a charity's work. Also, there is an average period of four years between the signing of the final will and death. An advertising campaign for legacies will therefore not bring quick results.

Legacy giving is as idiosyncratic as other aspects of charity giving. Half-remembered, half-understood information on the work of the charity can decide whether it is included in a will or not. The disproportionately high income of animal welfare charities from legacies can perhaps be explained by the neglect of the old people concerned by relatives and friends and by the companionship and devotion of their pets. Some might attribute it to senility. It does seem clear that it is not due to any exceptional advertising campaign by animal charities.

The legal aspect of legacies

It is very important to a charity that a legacy should be valid and not subject to dispute. To this end, it is usual for a charity to recommend a form of wording for bequests. An acceptable form of wording is:

FORM OF BEQUEST

I hereby bequeath the sum of........ pounds, to.......... .... (charity's name and address) .... and declare that the receipt of the Hon Secretary or Treasurer shall be a good discharge for the same.

It is important that the name of the charity is correct: if the charity is misdescribed, the executors may not be able to identify it, or they may divide the legacy between similarly named charities, or they may have to apply to the courts for an interpretation of the will.

If a charity receives a bequest and aggrieved relatives feel they have a claim on the estate, then the latter may take legal action. If the charity feels that the relatives have a moral, though not legal, claim, it cannot make an *ex gratia* payment (since a charity must use its income for the purpose for which it was given it), but can apply to the Charity Commissioners, who will approach the Attorney General, who has the power to authorize such payments.

There are different types of legacies. 'Straight legacies' are those in which there is a single payment. 'Residuary bequests' leave the residue of an estate after specific gifts have been made from it. 'Reversionary bequests' are those in which the testator bequeaths the income from his estate to someone, on whose death the estate becomes the property of the charity. Similarly, some bequests are made conditional on certain events (they are known as 'contingent interest bequests'), for example, a man may leave his estate to his wife, but in the event of her dying before him, he leaves it to a charity.

The charity cannot always spend a legacy at its own discretion. If a legacy is not bequeathed for a specific purpose (and this is usually the case), the charity can spend the money as it likes—for example, for administrative costs. If, however, a legacy is bequeathed on conditions, these must be adhered to. If the charity cannot agree to the conditions—for example, that it exercise racial discrimination in its disbursement of the legacy—then it can apply to the Charity Commissioners for a ruling of *cy près*, to get the conditions altered. It should also be noted that a charity has to spend a substantial part of its annual income or forfeit its entitlement to exemption from income tax—so a charity which receives an enormous legacy cannot invest it and use the interest to pay annual running costs.

Charities should avail themselves of the service previously offered by the Charities Department of the Principal Probate and Family Division, but now undertaken by Messrs Smee & Ford, by which any registered charity can be notified of any will of which it is a beneficiary and of any discretionary will of which it could possibly be a beneficiary. (A discretionary will is one in which the trustees can give to any charity at their discretion within a specified area of interest.) If your charity could benefit under a discretionary will, then send details of its work, which will constitute an appeal, to the trustees. There is no charge for a charity registering for this service, but the charity will be charged a modest fee for each notification. A registration form can be obtained from Messrs Smee & Ford, 6-7 New Bridge Street, London EC4.

Summary

Covenants and legacies can both be important sources of income to charities, although not every charity is equally able to secure these types of donations. In both cases the legal rules are stringent and must be observed. In particular, the administration of covenants, enabling the recovery of income tax, is complex—but a charity can use the services of the Charities Aid Foundation if it feels unable to undertake the administration of its own covenants.

To attract both covenants and legacies, a charity can advertise. It should make sure that its existing donors are fully aware of the possibilities of bequeathing money to the charity, and of covenanting donations.

6 House-to-house and street collections

Street collections are a very simple way to collect money for charity, involving a minimal amount of expense. A recent survey has shown that 90 per cent of the public give to charity only when directly asked by street or house-to-house collectors. Street collections remind people of a charity's existence and of the need for continuing support.

Collections can be of many types. They may be held on a house-to-house basis or by collectors who remain in one place. They may be straightforward requests for money, or involve the selling of flags (emblems) or goods (such as Christmas cards). They can include a service, such as carol singing, or none at all. Collections may be for money or for goods such as old clothing. They may involve the use of collecting boxes or previously delivered envelopes, or just individually issued receipts.

Legal regulations

All street and house-to-house collections must be authorized before they take place. A charity wishing to hold either a street collection (i.e. one in which funds are solicited on the public thoroughfare) or a house-to-house collection should write to the appropriate licensing authority, usually the Chief of Police for the area. (A list of licensing authorities is obtainable from the Home Office.) The application must be made at least a month before the proposed collection can take place (though the licensing authority can waive the rule in exceptional circumstances). In practice, a charity should normally apply at least a year in advance, as local authorities generally grant licences for flag days once a year. There is nothing to prevent a charity applying for a flag day at much shorter notice, on the off-chance of another charity's cancelling. Usually the licensing authority requires the charity to fill in its standard application form, but in any event the law stipulates that an application for a street or house-to-house collection must include the name of the promoter, the purpose of the collection, the locality to which it is to be confined, and dates within which it is to be carried out. It must state whether the proposed collection is house-to-house or a street collection, and whether flags are to be sold.

The police can refuse a licence or revoke one if:

(a) the proportion of expenses is too high (the average expenses for collections in London – which are expected to be higher than for other areas – is about 14 per cent. The cost of collecting boxes can be spread over several years);
(b) any collector or organizer is paying himself too generous a fee for his work;
(c) the collectors are, or are likely to be, disorderly;
(d) the applicant is an unsuitable person (e.g. a convicted criminal);
(e) the collectors are unfit (e.g. convicted criminals or under sixteen) and fail to comply with the regulations on the carrying of authorization badges;
(f) the charity fails to provide adequate information, which includes failure to complete the return form, which would preclude the granting of a permit in the future.

If the charity is refused a licence or a licence is revoked, the licensing authority will give written notice, stating their reasons, and the charity can appeal to the Home Secretary, within fourteen days. His decision is final. Often licensing authorities refuse applications simply because there are too many charities wanting to hold collections.

Exemption orders

If a national charity is likely to apply to hold a large number of house-to-house collections, in a large number of areas, the Home Office may issue an Exemption Order, which exempts the charity from having to apply for separate permission on each occasion. Fewer than 100 major charities hold Exemption Orders, and they are highly valued. They enable the charity's supporters to collect money or goods at any time, without prior permission. The charity usually informs the local licensing authority of its intentions to hold a collection, so that any overlapping, which annoys householders, can be avoided. An Exemption Order quite simply allows the charity to collect without prior permission—it does not exempt the charity from any other of the rules regulating house-to-house collections. An Exemption Order applies to house-to-house collections, not to street collections. It may be revoked if the charity fails to comply with the regulations governing house-to-house collections, or if the charity fails to hold sufficient collections to justify the use of an Exemption Order. (The most important consideration for the Home Office is that the charity should collect over a geographically wide area, in a substantial number of the 371 licensing authority areas.) If a charity risks losing its Exemption Order, the Home Office will warn the charity of its intention, to give it a chance to boost activity and thus not lose the Order. To apply for an Exemption Order, write to the Home Office and ask for an application form.

The organizer of a street or house-to-house collection is responsible for seeing that regulations are complied with. Briefly, these are that collectors must be sixteen years of age or over; each must carry two badges—one a certificate of authorization and one a prescribed badge—both of which bear the signature of the collector and that of the organizer. (Both badges must conform to Home Office regulations, which are included in the Home Office Regulations on House-to-House Collections.) Collectors must produce these badges on request, and must give their names to the police if asked. Collectors must not cause any annoyance to passers-by. Collecting boxes must be sealed, or if no box is used then receipts must be given from a receipt book with consecutively numbered pages. If envelopes are used (in a house-to-house collection), each envelope must have a gummed flap. Each box and authorization badge and permit issued should be listed by the organizer. The boxes should be numbered. Particular care should be taken to retrieve every box and authorization badge after the collection has been made.

When the collection has been completed, the boxes should be opened in the presence of the organizer and a witness, except if the sealed box is taken to the bank, when the organizer need not be present. The contents of each box should be listed. Envelopes, like collecting boxes, should be opened in front of a witness.

A statement of accounts has to be made to the licensing authority in the case of all collections. This shows the amount collected, the number of collecting boxes and if they have all been returned, and the expenses involved. Charities holding an Exemption Order have to make a return for all house-to-house collections held that year, one collection per form. A summary of accounts must be made both for collections of money and those for goods (such as old clothing).

It is important to understand and comply with the law on street and house-to-house collections. Although the punishments for breaking the law are small, the adverse publicity would be very damaging, and also precludes the charity's chances of securing a permit to hold a future collection.

Organizing a collection

This is a very different problem for a national charity (which wishes to ensure that it can hold collections throughout the country, perhaps on the same day, or within one week) and local charities or groups which have to cover only one area. For the national charity, the first question is whether to try for flag days and house-to-house collections on one day, or whether to stagger the collections throughout the year. Some charities have traditionally collected throughout the country in a concentrated period—most notably Poppy Day (Royal British Legion Poppy Appeal) and Christian Aid Week. The licensing authority will reserve the desired dates for them year after year. But for charities with no tradition of a nationwide collection day, the disadvantages of holding one should be considered. They require a larger number of staff than a campaign spread throughout the year—after all, one person cannot be everywhere at the same time, or co-ordinate 1,000 collections all on the same day. One runs the risk of bad weather, which will adversely affect the success of the collection, influencing not only the number of collectors prepared to venture out but also the good temper and disposition of the donors. Imagine the misery of the charity which worked all year round on a week's national house-to-house collection and a national flag day, to find its collectors snowed in. There are variations in local conditions, which a national collection, concentrated within a very limited period, cannot take account of. What is a good day to collect on in Weston super Mare may be a rotten day on which to collect in Manchester.

The main advantage of a concentrated collection is the publicity impact. A charity can advertise, prepare the public for the campaign and hold stunts for the national press—ranging from personalities giving to collectors to bunny girls shaking cans. In fact, a charity's ability to hold a national fund-raising day or week depends on its having a great deal of support, throughout the country, so that it can mobilize an army of collectors. Having a large number of groups does not mean that they will all be able, or prepared, to support a national day: much will depend on their subservience to headquarters.

If the charity does not have a date for its collections fixed by tradition, such as Poppy Day, then it should state its preference when applying. Because of the limited number of dates available, the licensing authority may not be able to allocate the requested day, but will take it as a guideline. In choosing a date, bear in mind likely weather conditions. August may be a dud month in an industrial town, but it could be very rewarding at a seaside resort.

Joint flag days

Some charities group together to hold street collections for their various causes. It is usual for the charities to work in related fields—for example, for the blind, or children, or the aged. The proceeds can be divided amongst the participating charities, either in proportion to the number of collectors each provides, or so that the charity keeps the money collected by its collectors. The first case recognizes that not all sites are equally lucrative. In both cases charities are expected to share the costs of the collection. If taking part in an amalgamated collection, a charity should ensure that, in fact, one person is in overall charge, co-ordinating the individual charities' collectors, and responsible for seeing that legal requirements are complied with. This one person should also be responsible for ordering 'flags' and collecting boxes.

It is argued by some charities that these joint flag days or house-to-house collections are of great benefit, since they reduce the duplication of collections, which the public finds irritating. This seems dubious reasoning—people can refuse to give: they should not begrudge others the opportunity to do so. Since a majority of the population gives to charity only when confronted by a collector, it is hard to avoid the conclusion that charities should hold more street collections. It should be remembered by collectors and the general public that those in need of charity have more to trouble them than the irritation of being called to answer the door twice a week to collectors, or the inconvenience of avoiding flag sellers on street corners. In fact, it must be very unusual for anyone to be asked to give as often as fifty times a year. What bunching of appeals there is happens most with carol-singing, around Christmas time, and is a seasonal hazard, like canvassers at election time.

Amalgamated collections are of most value to small, lesser known charities, which would not normally be able to organize their own collections, lacking both sufficient support to enlist enough collectors and, since unknown to the public, unlikely to secure a good response. By participating in a collection with other charities in the same field, the small charity has access to this relatively simple method of fund-raising.

One factor which should be considered by the larger charity considering amalgamating for a flag day or collection is that, by not having the charity's name on the flags and boxes (but rather a common name, like Alexandra Rose Day), the charity loses some of the publicity value of the collection: its name is not placed before the hundreds of passers-by.

Getting collectors

The more collectors there are the more money will be raised, so a major part of the charity's effort should go on recruiting collectors. If a national charity has a group in the area, then its members, their families and friends should provide the nucleus of collectors. Supporters on the mailing list can also be invited to give a couple of hours of their time. A letter should be sent to the local press, preferably signed by some local dignitary, such as the Mayor, informing people that a collection is to be made, and asking both for a generous response and for volunteers to act as collectors. Some charities, usually those with a national flag day, place large advertisements in the papers asking for collectors. Of course, other forms of publicity, such as posters in local shops, should also be used.

Contact should be made with local groups, such as women's organizations, asking them if their supporters could help. The local town hall can usually provide a list of local organizations. The sixth-formers of local schools are often willing collectors, as are members of the local youth clubs (but legally collectors must not be under sixteen). University students or those at local technical colleges can be exceptionally enthusiastic collectors—to mobilize them, contact the Student Union, or the appropriate society (the Student Union will usually be able to tell you the name of the person you need to contact).

It is very important, when recruiting collectors, not to make collecting sound a depressing task. It can be fun. Emphasize that you are asking for only a few hours' work, probably once a year, and emphasize how much help can be given as a result of the money raised.

Collectors should be well briefed on the charity's work, because some people may ask what the money is being solicited for, and they have a right to a coherent answer. As collectors must also know the legal position governing their behaviour as collectors, it is generally convenient to have a briefing session before the collection begins or, if this is not practicable, for the charity to issue a sheet of instruction, with a summary of the charity's work.

Some collectors are more successful than others. Not surprisingly, attractive girls get more donations than men. All collectors should be a credit to the charity—a clean collector is likely to collect more than a scruffy one. Usually collectors realize this, but if the problem seems likely to arise, a very tactful reminder is unlikely to alienate anyone. It does a charity's image good to be seen to attract collectors from all walks of life, and different ethnic backgrounds.

Most collectors like to work in pairs, if collecting house-to-house, doing one side of the road each, giving each other moral support. When collecting on a public thoroughfare, collectors should work singly, to avoid blocking the pavement.

Types of collecting box

These vary enormously. Though a collection may be made without a box, if receipts are issued, it is less usual, and not usually practicable—it slows up the procedure too much. Boxes may be disposable, used only once, then cut open and thrown away. Since they are in fact destroyed by being opened they have the great advantage of reducing fraud (a dishonest collector cannot open the box and then close it again). Disposable boxes are more expensive in the long run than re-usable boxes, though they can be economically viable where a collection in a certain area involves the use of a large number of boxes which would subsequently have to be returned to the charity's headquarters rather than retained by the group for future use. The high rate of postal charges makes the disposable boxes cheaper for this type of situation.

Re-usable boxes can be metal or plastic—the latter is lighter and more convenient. The charity will, on top of the purchasing price of the boxes, have to meet the running cost of re-seal labels, usually printed with the charity's name, and name labels for the box. Specialist suppliers of collecting box materials charge the least for this type of printing. Most charities use boxes of standard design, and have distinctive colours or labels, but a charity can, if it wishes, commission a specially designed box.

Other than boxes, a charity can use envelopes, delivering them house-to-house and arranging for a later pick-up. This method involves twice the work in terms of walking, but reduces the time spent at each house explaining the purpose of the call. But people might be tempted to put less in an envelope than they might put in a box under the scrutiny of a collector.

Mention should also be made of the statuette-type collecting box most usually seen outside chemists' shops. These have to be specially designed for the charity, and are expensive to purchase (over £20 each). A charity can, over time, recoup the cost of the statuette, but must also consider that it will incur the costs involved in emptying the box at frequent intervals. Even if this is done by a volunteer, the charity should consider if this is the most fruitful use of their time. The placing of these statuettes is crucial to their success: a well-placed one may yield as much as £150 a year, another as little as £5; the average is around £20 a year.

Collecting boxes with movable parts are often very attractive to children, but can require a great deal of maintenance. Children are the most usual donors: they enjoy feeding small coins in statuette collecting boxes, and this should be borne in mind when having such boxes designed. Ordinary collecting boxes can be placed on shop counters, but the problems of regular collection should be considered before the enthusiastic distribution of boxes. All boxes not in the charge of collectors should be well secured, so that the risk of theft is reduced.

Suppliers of collecting boxes, statuettes, flags and other collecting devices usually make themselves known to charities, by soliciting trade. Pre-eminent is Angal Collecting Boxes and Devices Ltd, of

London, which designs most of the statuettes and supplies a large range of boxes.

Where to collect

As well as the attractiveness of the collectors, the location of the collection is crucial in determining its success. In street collections, obviously, the busier the street the more potential donors there are. Outside railway stations is a good place, as well as shopping precincts and busy street corners. The best positions are those in which people are not too busy to stop—for this reason stations in shopping areas are usually better than the commuter stations. It is usually fairly obvious to local people which are the key sites—ask them to rank them, and cover them all in order of likely profitability, if shortage of collectors means that they cannot all be covered. Obviously not all areas are busy all the time, and this must be taken into account.

When collecting under a house-to-house licence, one is not, in fact, limited to collecting literally house-to-house, but merely confined to collecting on private property. This means that one can, with the landlord's consent, collect in pubs. People often feel slightly guilty about spending money on drink, and consequently respond generously to collections in pubs. A pub collection can yield the highest results of any kind of collection, and in a very short time. It is often a very attractive form of collection to students and other people, so the problem of recruiting collectors is reduced—but not all volunteers would be prepared to collect in pubs. When collecting house-to-house, if shortage of collectors means that not every house in the area can be covered, then avoid houses with long drives (although they may be thought to yield the highest profits, because of the imagined wealth of the occupant). The amount that people put into collecting boxes varies surprisingly little, irrespective of their wealth.

Carol singing

Collections under a house-to-house or street licence can both be made by carol singers. Carol singers can be under sixteen, but in that case must be accompanied by adults, who do the actual collecting. To recruit carol singers, try the local church or school choirs or the local youth clubs. (See p. 45 for carol singing by young people. Do not forget the possibility of sponsored carol singing.) Carol singers must carry permits and authorization badges. It is sensible to give them all a duplicated sheet of the words of the carols.

It is much more time consuming to carol sing house-to-house than just to collect, since each household expects at least one carol. It is usually more profitable to collect on a busy thoroughfare, under a street collection licence, or in a station or grouped round the town's Christmas tree. Carol singers can collect substantial amounts, as passers-by feel they are rewarding effort, as well as giving to charity.

Sale of flags

People respond better to a street collection where flags are being sold. It gives them something for their money. By wearing the emblem, they avoid the hostility of collectors they subsequently meet, and they are not importuned again. Flags can be obtained from the same suppliers as collecting boxes. Flags should be kept simple, to keep costs down. There are plain, standard designs which can be overprinted with the charity's name, though the charity can commission its own flags. All sorts of tricksy devices are available for flag sellers, ranging from fancy trays to plastic flag dispensers. Many have been designed to fill non-existent needs, and common sense should be exercised in ordering them. Remember, a collector is on duty for probably two hours at a time, not for days on end, so devices to ease the burden of the flags and collecting box are scarcely necessary.

Collecting goods house-to-house

Successful collections of goods, such as old clothes and blankets, can be made house-to-house. Sacks should be delivered with a covering label, asking for contributions to be put in the sack and either left outside the door for collection on a specified day, or to be called for at a specified time. It is important to call back at the time stated, as otherwise a great deal of ill will would accrue to the charity. Householders can be asked for donations at the same time —if it is convenient to do so. (See also pp. 120–2 on trading and thrift shops.)

Selling

Charities can sell goods on a house-to-house basis, under a house-to-house licence, but a substantial amount of the money collected must go to the charity. A recent judgment showed that 16 per cent of the proceeds was not a suitably large enough amount to warrant the description as a charity collection. The most suitable items for selling door-to-door are the charity's publications and its Christmas cards. But remember that it is easier for people to refuse to buy something that they do not want, than to refuse to give a donation to charity.

Summary

The main points to note are that flag days and house-to-house collections are extremely profitable. The stringent legal restrictions must be complied with, and no unauthorized collection must take place. Cheerful, courteous collectors can do much for a charity's image, as well as boost takings. Collections can be made for goods as well as money. Donations can be placed in boxes or envelopes or individual receipts can be issued. Carol singing can take place both under a house-to-house and a street collection licence. The choice of site is crucial to the success of the collection. Pubs are amongst the most profitable sites. To recruit volunteers to act as collectors, try local organizations such as women's groups, youth clubs, schools, colleges and university. Do not make collecting sound like a drudge: emphasize that it can be fun. Consider concentrating your collections on one day or week only if your charity has sufficient national support and the administrative capacity. Do not forget to make a return (showing the accounts) to the licensing authority: it is required by law.

7 Functions

Charities organize glittering film premieres or balls in the mistaken belief that such schemes yield huge profits. In fact, nothing could be further from the truth. Charities lose more money over concerts and balls and film premieres than over any other events. Even when profits are made they are rarely commensurate with the amount of effort expended.

The reasons for losses on functions are varied, but fall into three main categories: first, problems in selling tickets; second, inaccurate costings; and third, huge overheads.

1. *Problems in selling tickets*

Before committing itself to any expenditure, the charity must work out precisely the measure of support that it can count on. To do this, ask committee members how many tickets they will buy, or undertake to sell, and if they are prepared to guarantee this number. Take only the number which they guarantee as firm—treat the rest as bragging. If the number of guaranteed tickets is sufficient to meet costs, then the charity can proceed with confidence. All ticket revenues over those guaranteed constitute the profit.

In some cases ticket sales cannot be planned in this way—for example, for a pop concert (when the charity is acting as an entrepreneur). Be especially cautious where prior commitment to buy tickets does not cover cost: it is these situations where the charity stands to lose most money.

Unforeseen difficulties may arise in selling the tickets—the event may not be as popular as those planning it supposed (this is a very common fault—the organizer supposes that because he enjoys dinner dances with speeches everyone else does). The event may be outdoor, and the weather poor in the weeks preceding it. The tickets may be too expensive. There is usually a limit to how much people are prepared to pay for an evening out. The problem for the charity is that if people pay £10 for a ticket to a charity ball they think they are making a generous donation to the charity. In fact, they are paying £5 to the caterer, £1 to the band, £2 for the hire of the hall, £1.50 for printing, postage and other overheads, and perhaps 50p to the charity.

Some charities are fortunate enough to have firmly committed supporters who will buy tickets for all of its functions; others have an annual ball or concert which has built up a strong following; but for most charities, each function brings the problem of selling tickets. Who will sell the tickets, and to whom? Can many be sold through advertising? Is ticket selling going to turn into a nightmare, occupying the time of paid staff and thus eroding profit? All these questions should be discussed before the charity commits itself to holding a function. Two weeks before a ball is not the time to worry about selling tickets to cover the £2,000 overheads.

Ticket selling is not so difficult if the event is organized by a group or aid committee. The group's members will buy tickets themselves and sell them to family, friends, neighbours and colleagues, many of whom will exact retribution by selling tickets to similar events. The ticket selling is thus done on a knock-for-knock basis, and charity events become part of the community's social life.

It is a very different matter for the charity's staff to undertake the ticket selling, except where a regular clientele has been built up so that the task of ticket selling becomes merely administrative. Since few charity workers are well paid, few of them are likely to be able to afford the tickets or have friends who might. (There are notable exceptions, as some charities have traditionally employed debutantes at low pay.) If a charity wants to organize a function, it would do well to consider setting up a committee specially for the event, whose main task would be ticket selling and securing advertisements for the souvenir brochure (see below). The members of the charity's board of trustees or their wives might provide a base from which to evolve a committee.

National charities most frequently find themselves tempted into the promotion of special events in London, so the headquarters staff take on many of the jobs that a local group would do in the provinces. For many events the organization can be done splendidly by headquarters staff, but as a general rule ticket selling should be done by volunteers with backgrounds appropriate to the event.

2. *Inaccurate costing*

Many charities have watched with dismay their supposed profits being eroded by unforeseen expenses. When planning an event work out all the likely expenses. Make a generous allowance for those where the precise figures are not known. Ask for a quotation from the ballroom owner, caterer, band, theatre proprietor, etc., if possible in writing. If a written quotation is not given, write down figures agreed verbally: do not rely on memory. Ask several times if there are likely to be any other expenses. Too often the extra costs of cloakroom attendants and porters and taxis home for the staff after midnight are conveniently overlooked when the price is being quoted.

When you have some idea of the likely costs, sit down and draw up a costing sheet (see next page). This means listing all likely expenses (and should include hire of the hall, cost of entertainers, food, drink, lighting and heating, printing costs, stationery, postage, advertising and any other costs) and showing the likely revenue if the tickets are sold at various prices, with varying numbers sold. This should show the possible profits.

3. *Large overheads lead to losses*

Avoid like poison anything that requires a large prior commitment of funds. What is 'large' must depend on the charity's income and resources. A charity which organizes an event with high overheads, with no guarantee of covering them, must realize that it is using its funds, given for charitable purposes, as risk capital. A charity must not speculate to accumulate.

If a function involves a large outlay, think of another type of event that does not—or try to get the person requiring the money to share the risk, and waive the fee if the event is a failure. Charities should be aware of the lack of scruple used by some, who will exact a deposit from the charity, and contrive not to return it, on many trumped-up reasons.

If there is only a small outlay, then there can only be a small loss. When the amount to be spent reaches four figures, make sure there is enough in hand from advance ticket sales to cover the costs. A moment's reflection on the grimness of having to explain away a loss of over £1,000 at an annual general meeting of supporters should serve as a brake on undertaking high overheads.

COSTING SHEET FOR A CHARITY BALL

(Based on actual figures for a ball given in aid of a housing aid centre, June 1975.)

Hire of hall with bar facilities, 2 discos and DJs (to include all overheads and full staff)		
Catering (menu agreed) + glass of wine (for 700 guests)		£1,109 (+ VAT)
for every additional 100 guests the cost of food and drink		£119 (+ VAT)
Group: Nasty Means		£125 (+ VAT)
Printing: ticket application forms and tickets		£46
Stationery		£15
Postage: ticket applications and tickets		£75
Costs:	for 700 guests	£1,370 (+ VAT)
	for 800 guests	£1,489 (+ VAT)
	for 900 guests	£1,608 (+ VAT)
	for 1,000 guests	£1,717 (+ VAT)

Revenue—if tickets are £4 a head:

200 tickets	£800	
300 tickets	£1,200	
400 tickets	£1,600	
		roughly break-even point
500 tickets	£2,000	
700 tickets	£2,800	
800 tickets	£3,200	
900 tickets	£3,600	
1,000 tickets	£4,000	

If tickets are £3.50, then break-even point is reached at about 440 tickets.

Note: Losses will be made if ticket sales do not reach 400.

These costings make no allowance for any additional income, like tombola or programme revenue.

Those are some 'don'ts'. There is one big 'do' – use the event as an occasion for other fund-raising devices. The main profit from a function usually comes from the programme, tombola, raffle and other peripheral events.

1. *The programme or souvenir brochure*

The function rarely needs a programme, and so it is generally referred to as the souvenir brochure. There is usually a page or two of editorial (describing the charity's work, appealing for further funds and thanking supporters) but the bulk of the programme is taken up with advertisements from well-wishers. Individuals can advertise (usually using the wording, 'Best wishes for the work of X charity from Mr and Mrs John Smith'), as can firms.

Advertising in charity brochures is a recognized way of giving for firms, and many have budgets specifically for this purpose. To secure advertisements, appoint a programme sub-committee, whose members will approach friends and business colleagues for support. In choosing members for this committee, remember that the right attitude can be more useful than the right contacts: people must not be too embarrassed to ask for advertising and must be able to think of those who will benefit as a result of their efforts rather than the possible damage a refusal will do to their egos.

A letter, signed by either the president or chairman of the charity or the chairman of the programme committee, should be prepared. It should include information on the charity's work (i.e. why the appeal is being made), information on the event for which the programme is being prepared, and a request for support. Potential advertisers should be told that their support will generate goodwill for their company as well as advertising its products. An order form should be included, showing the sizes of advertising space being offered, and specifications for printing (whether blocks or artwork are required). It is sensible to include requests for donations, tombola and raffle prizes, etc. on the advertising order form, in an attempt to maximize the effectiveness of the mailing.

The letter should be sent to large companies, local firms and those likely to be sympathetic to the cause (for example, children's charities should approach toy and childswear manufacturers). (See pp. 70–1 for details on how to compile a list of firms for a mailing.) Personal approaches should be made by programme committee members to businessmen known to them. Many approaches will have to be made to secure a good response. It is hard to generalize (some causes are more popular than others) but certainly a 10 per cent favourable response would be exceptionally good, and 2–3 per cent more usual.

The amount to charge for each advertisement depends on what the market will bear. £100 a page is about average for a major charity's London event, but rates can vary from £20 a page to £500. Make sure before fixing the price that you know what each page will, in fact, cost to produce. Ask for estimates from several printers, giving several possible numbers of pages. Assume that you will want to have enough copies to sell at the function itself and to send voucher copies to the advertisers. The programme can be given away to those attending the function, or it can be sold for a fixed or unspecified amount. Pretty girls are the best programme sellers.

2. *Raffles*

For raffles, see Chapter 1, pp. 34–6.

One point to note is that the prizes should be appropriate to the event. They should not be the same for an audience of sixty-year-olds and one of twenty-year-olds.

3. *Tombolas*

For information on tombolas, see Chapter 1, p. 29.

The display of tombola prizes should be as attractive as possible, to tempt buyers. Requests to buy tickets should be cheerful and never deteriorate into bullying. If people feel chivvied, they will avoid your functions in the future.

There are many other side events which may be incorporated into a function—see the section on Bazaars, pp. 28–9.

Individual functions—and some of their problems

Film premieres

The charity takes over the cinema for the premiere of a film, and becomes responsible for all that evening's costs. For its profits, it relies on its supporters paying a premium price for the seats. Their reasons for doing so may be complex—it may be to support the charity, a cause which they feel commitment toward; it may be for the glamour of the occasion, especially where the event is graced by royalty; sometimes it is argued that holding lavish events for charity enables participants to overcome guilt about indulging themselves.

To hold a film premiere, the charity should contact one of the large film companies and ask if they have any suitable films coming up. There is a queue of charities for the best films. In some cases charities will take the third or fourth night of the film, as other charities have already been awarded rights to the first and second nights. It helps a charity to secure a film premiere from the film companies if they can hold out the lure of a royal patron, and the chance of a Royal Film Performance, as this helps publicize the film, which is what the film company is interested in. The charity will often be offered the film free of charge, but still has to meet the costs of the cinema hire and staff. It is sensible to arrange with the cinema that they will handle the routine box office sales, especially of the lower price tickets.

Theatre premieres

These are less usual than film premieres because the prior publicity for the theatre is not as extensive as for the cinema, so that people tend to wait for the reviews before rushing to buy tickets; theatres are generally much smaller than cinemas, so the economics of theatre premieres are not so attractive; live performances involve higher overheads than film shows, which further reduces profitability; theatre management are reluctant to give charities good nights, with a chance of selling the seats, and tend to offer rainy Mondays. It is hard to organize a satisfactory theatre premiere, because even if one can secure the agreement of the theatre management, and all the performers, one has to sell the tickets at a premium, and be confident of a full house. The main profit will come from the souvenir brochure, but a theatre premiere does not lend itself well to other side events, although a raffle or tombola can be set up in the foyer, if fire regulations allow.

Organizing one's own show or pop concert

One can try to organize a show oneself—hiring the theatre, coaxing stars to perform, as well as selling the tickets and organizing the programme. It is clearly easier to take on a ready-organized show than to organize one from scratch. But the individually organized show may be outstandingly popular—like Frank Sinatra or the Rolling Stones—and consequently high prices may be charged.

In some circumstances, charities are approached by individual 'artistes' offering their services, and they may be sufficiently well known to be able to attract enough co-stars to build up a show. This can be ideal—but beware the second-rate performers who want to exploit the charity. Make clear that no fee is offered and that 'expenses' does not mean a non-taxable fee but only reimbursement of actual expenses incurred.

Individual artists can be approached through their agents. (The BBC will normally be able to furnish the name and address of an artist's agent.) But it is better if you can approach artists personally. They may be listed with their address in *Who's Who*. Asking around other artists, agents and concert promoters often yields addresses and phone numbers of specific artists. People are generally helpful to charities, so explain what you want and they will try to help if they can. It is wrong to believe that you have to know people to get them to do anything for charity.

In organizing a show or a concert, one is taking a gamble on what will be popular and draw an audience. If your charity has regular supporters, then you may have some idea of what type of show would appeal to them, or has been successful in the past, and can cater accordingly. In promoting pop concerts, it is unlikely that the charity will be relying on its supporters to buy tickets, but rather that they will rely on the general appeal of the performers to attract an audience. Organizing pop concerts is recognized by those doing it to be a tricky business—witness all the newspaper stories of concerts which lose thousands of pounds. Not only do tastes change rapidly, but also there are vast regional variations in pop concert tastes. One charity was greatly chagrined to hear that a pop group's concert in Birmingham had drawn crowds of thousands, whereas its own concert in London by the same group had a few weeks previously drawn an audience of 200. Capacity audiences for pop concerts do not always mean a profit. Pop groups, and those letting the halls for such concerts, have become notorious for their habits of escalating expenses. As a general rule, it is always sensible to hold concerts at a venue which has an established clientele for such events, as this will take care of the bulk of the ticket selling. But it is fair to say that those running such halls are aware of their strength, and see charities' dependence on them as providing a chance of profit—though they usually are the most verbose in protesting their affection and deep sympathy for the charity's cause. Perhaps one might say that fund-raisers promoting pop concerts for charity feel that even where it was profitable it was not usually worth the headache.

Auctions and sales

Pictures, antiques, jewellery and silver are amongst the items that a charity can collect for sale or auction. With an auction, the buyers must all be there at one specific time, so the charity should consider if it can rely on its supporters to attend, and buy, or if it has goods of sufficient calibre to attract dealers and collectors. A sale, over several days, means that more people have the opportunity to attend, but it also means that the site has to be staffed and a hall hired for its duration. An auction or sale can be combined with a social event, such as a wine and cheese party, especially if the items are not of very high quality and will not be very expensive.

Items can also be sold on a tombola system. Each item is numbered, and tickets are sold up to the number of items (i.e. 100 tickets for 100 items). All tickets are put into a hat and as they are drawn the ticket holder can choose the item wanted. This type of sale is held very successfully by the Ben Uri Art Gallery, London. The tickets are not cheap (about £20) but one stands the chance of gaining a Chagall original—though one also risks getting something very inferior!

To set up an auction, contact a local auctioneer and ask one of the partners if he would be willing to give his services free for the occasion. It is unusual to be refused. He will also advise you if any of the items are of great value and should not be sold below a certain price. In choosing a place to hold the auction, aim at somewhere convenient, where the goods can be suitably displayed and, if possible, one which has an established trade with buyers and known collectors. For example, an art gallery is ideal for an art sale, and often non-commercial galleries are very sympathetic. The main advantage of using an established venue is that one can use the mailing list and thus reach likely buyers.

To collect goods for a sale, approach supporters, write to the local paper asking for contributions, ask shops and galleries in the area, write to famous individuals and known collectors, and do not forget those old standbys, family and friends. It is surprising how much bric-a-brac, silver and jewellery one can gather from these sources. If collecting pictures or cartoons, then try the artists, who are often very generous in donating work. Their addresses are generally to be found in *The Artist's Year Book*. Cartoonists can be contacted via the papers and magazines that publish their work. Often artists are happy to arrange profit sharing sales with the charity. They benefit by having their work shown, often to a new audience, and the charity stands to gain part of the proceeds. When asking for items for sale, whether pictures or antiques, a charity should make the cause seem urgent, and clear indication should be given of how the proceeds will be spent.

A successful sale or auction must depend on attracting sufficient buyers. All usual forms of publicity should be used—posters, advertisements in the local and specialist papers, letters to the local press and, if appropriate (i.e. sufficiently newsworthy), a press release. Contact dealers: they are serious buyers. At one silver sale in London, everything was sold to dealers within ten minutes of opening, to the consternation of latecomers and the bewilderment of the organizers.

You can charge an admission fee to a sale or an auction, but the amount should be modest, so as not to deter clients. Save any unsold items for a future sale, or for a bazaar, or for gifts in a tombola. If any item of obvious worth is unsold, or fails to reach an adequate price at auction, then consider sending it to a reputable auction room. Of course one has to take a risk at any auction that the item will not reach a fair price. Selling items too cheaply will alienate the donors; selling them too expensively will alienate the buyers; so it is important to try to strike a balance.

The success of a sale will depend on attracting valuable items and sufficient buyers. A sale of antiques may be an enormous success in one town and draw no buyers in another—it is a question of judgment to choose the right type of goods for the area. In other words, do not assume that because one charity makes thousands of pounds with a sale of antique jewellery that your charity will automatically have a similar success. Sometimes a charity thinks up a new type of sale—for example, War On Want held the first large-scale cartoon sale—and finds an enormous market; but sometimes goods have not been sold before because there is no market for them.

Balls, dinners and dances

In many communities balls, dinners and dances are an established part of the social life, and are a recognized meeting ground for young people. In these circumstances it is sensible to organize such events, for a measure of support may be expected. It is very difficult to organize a successful ball or dinner if no obvious constituency exists.

Presupposing that the charity is confident of support and so decides to go ahead and organize the event, special care must be taken over the costing—because the costs, especially if there is catering, will be high. People expect value for money and will be annoyed if they fail to get it, and this is difficult for the charity to achieve in a period of rapid price rises. Some charities have abandoned their balls because of rising costs, and others do not charge for the ticket, but rather make an on-the-spot appeal for funds. The charity has to be very confident of its supporters' generosity to be able to do this.

Balls and dinners at which these public appeals are made (and at which people's donations are publicly announced) are the most rewarding in fund-raising terms. People are shamed into giving generously. But whilst this practice is acceptable in some circles, in others it would be greatly resented and would become counter-productive—people would avoid going to such functions again. If organizing an on-the-spot appeal, make sure that those attending are expecting one. Have a good, emotional speaker making the appeal, who will pull at the heart strings. Keep the speech short. The appeal must be kept good humoured—the audience must not be berated for a miserly response, but rather congratulated on its generosity, whether or not it is generous. It is helpful to have some key members of the audience (committee members and past committee members) approached before the meeting, and asked to set the pace—to announce their contributions to set the ball rolling, and also set high standards of generosity. Appeals at dinners are quite usual. The event should be made attractive by the presence of distinguished guests and interesting after-dinner speakers.

For balls and dances for young people, try to choose a novel location or theme. Riverboat shuffles, although suffering the risk of bad weather, may prove attractive, as may dances in an old tithe barn or other unusual place. If the place is not a particular attraction, then try to devise a theme that is either seasonal or national.

See if it is possible to organize a cabaret, or promise an evening with the stars and coax celebrities to attend. You have to offer people more for their money than just a dinner or dance, since you will be charging them for more, to make a profit. Souvenir brochures and raffles and tombolas should all be used to boost revenue.

Summary

Balls, theatre and film premieres, pop concerts, art sales, antique auctions can all be held to raise funds. They are most successful when organized on behalf of a charity by an aid committee whose members will sell the tickets. Great care should be taken to avoid large overheads, which could result in a considerable expense to the charity if the function is a flop. Consider how and to whom tickets will be sold before organizing the event. Prepare an accurate costing. Boost revenue by organizing a souvenir brochure, a raffle and a tombola. Above all, think long and hard before holding a function: not only can it fail to make a profit, it can also be a money-loser.

8 Trading

Increasingly, charities are turning to trading as a way of boosting their incomes, calculating that it is easier to sell something than simply to ask for a donation. In fact, although the charity may, through sales, raise funds from those who might not otherwise normally support it, people find it harder to refuse direct requests for help, than to decline to buy something that they might neither need nor like. So, in trading, a charity must be aware that its success depends on its ability to select the right things for sale. Also, a charity must be jealous of its good name and adopt rigorously high moral standards in its trading.

Legal position

The law regulating the trading activities of charities is vague. A charity cannot trade as its primary object and retain its charitable status, but there is no precise ruling on how much a charity can trade, judged either by size of turnover or proportion of its income, before it can be said to be trading as its primary object. It is in no way illegal for charities to trade; simply that they cannot expect tax exemption on their trading activities, which would be obtainable on their other activities (see below for the tax position of charity trading).

Generally, charities are cautious and trade through a trading subsidiary, which covenants all its profits to the charity, which then reclaims the tax. A charity running one or two temporary thrift shops, or selling Christmas cards to its supporters on a modest scale, would probably not need to operate through a trading subsidiary; but since the matter is subject to interpretation, legal advice can be sought—or the Charity Commissioners will give their advice free of charge. A charity which is considered by the Charity Commissioners to be in danger of becoming over-involved in trading, so that trading is its primary object, would be warned accordingly. No action would be taken in the first instance, so that the charity concerned would have the chance to rectify the situation, either by reducing its trading activities or by forming a trading subsidiary.

Tax position

The tax liability on a charity's trading activities is complex. Generally, a charity cannot expect the tax concessions applicable to its usual activities to extend to its trading, except in certain circumstances. For example, if the profits are for the purpose of the charity and the trade is carried out by the beneficiaries of the charity as well, then there is exemption from corporation tax. Thus gifts or Christmas cards made by the disabled in sheltered workshops, with the profits accruing to the charity, would qualify for exemption.

Through an extra-statutory concession by the Inland Revenue, the sale of goods at bazaars and jumble sales are exempt from corporation tax as long as (a) the charity is not regularly trading, (b) the trading is not in competition with other traders, (c) the profits are for the charity, and (d) the public supports the venture because the profits go to charity.

Whereas the premises occupied by a charity are allowed a reduction of 50 per cent of rates, and greater relief at the discretion of the local authority, no such concession is allowed on premises which the charity uses for trading (such as a thrift shop), as this is not the primary purpose of the charity.

Charities when trading are not generally excluded from the obligation to pay VAT, but the liability to pay VAT is not reached until gross takings are in excess of £5,000 p.a. Certain concessions have been made to charities, such as the zero rating of second-hand goods donated for sale, and on new goods donated for sale up to a limit of £10. A charity liable to VAT should register, and make quarterly returns, claiming 'input' (i.e. the costs which can be offset against the final VAT liability) and showing the amount to be paid. A useful guide to the charity's liability to VAT is obtainable from the National Council of Social Service (26 Bedford Square, London WC1), and a second guide from the same organization gives details on how to account for VAT. Charities with any queries about VAT liability can contact Customs and Excise, VAT Liability, Division D, Atlantic House, Holborn Viaduct, London EC1.

To avoid VAT liability, some charities attempt to differentiate between various activities, which would otherwise be liable to VAT, and make them the responsibility of different bodies, so that gross turnover will not reach £5,000 p.a. For example, a national charity may make its branches and aid committees independent for this purpose. Careful thought needs to be given to such a step, as the branches or committees must retain a considerable measure of independence if they are to satisfy the Customs and Excise that they are indeed separate organizations, and this may not suit the parent body.

VAT collection is regarded as onerous by charities, and local groups often find the degree of administration required deters them from undertaking trading activities as enthusiastically as otherwise. To overcome this problem it is sometimes possible for a national charity to persuade Customs and Excise to regard the charity's local groups as agents, which enables the national charity to undertake VAT collection centrally and thus relieve the groups of the administration. The local groups are given a set price at which to sell an article, and send the proceeds to headquarters; they do not have to deduct VAT and send it to Customs and Excise—this is done for them.

What to sell, how, and to whom

There are no restrictions on the goods that a charity can offer for sale, although it should operate within the bounds of good taste. Some goods are traditionally associated with charity trading, such as Christmas cards or baskets made by the blind, and members of the public will even seek out such goods when planning their purchase.

Christmas and greetings cards

Most major charities sell Christmas cards, and many smaller

charities are tempted into this apparently lucrative field. But whilst sales of Christmas cards can be very profitable, the success of the operation depends on several factors. First, per unit cards yield a very low profit; therefore worthwhile profits depend on selling large numbers of cards. The five charities which sell the most Christmas cards reach a turnover of between £200,000 and £1 million each, of which about 40 per cent is profit. This level of profit is achieved because the number of cards ordered reduces the cost per card, whereas the charity selling fewer cards will face a much higher unit cost, which reduces profit margins to as little as 5 or 10 per cent. Many small charities feel that the publicity value of having Christmas cards, carrying their name to a wider public, outweighs considerations of profitability.

The choice of design, together with the popularity of the charity's cause, are only part of the reason for a charity's success in the charity Christmas cards business. More important than either seems to be the efficiency of the marketing operation. There are a variety of ways of selling Christmas cards, and the successful charity will exploit them all. The basis of the sales will be made up by sales to supporters. This does not mean the bulk of sales, but that there should be a basic level of sales to supporters, which will pay for the cost of the operation and assure that all additional sales are profitable. The Charity Christmas Card Council (see below) advise that any charity hoping to enter the Christmas cards field should have a minimum of 6,000 donors on their mailing list, to provide a hard core of customers. The charity's groups and supporters should be encouraged to sell the cards at bazaars and fêtes and to their friends. This can be surprisingly important: the National Society for the Mentally Handicapped Child sells the bulk of its £1 million worth of cards and gifts through its groups and supporters. If the charity has thrift shops, then they provide a valuable sales outlet for the cards; for example, the major outlet for Oxfam cards is Oxfam thrift shops. It is usual for the larger charities to produce mail order leaflets, illustrating the available designs, and these are sent not only to those on the donor file but also to enquirers, past customers, the press and the media. (The high cost of postage makes it sensible to combine the mail order leaflet with any Christmas appeal literature which the charity may be planning.)

National charities may also take advantage of the Charity

Christmas Card Council scheme, which provides a joint marketing operation for charity Christmas cards. Over 100 charities belong to the Council, which will accept as a member any registered charity which is national. Each member is charged a fee, based on the size of sales, those with the greatest turnover paying about £70, those with the smallest about £15. The Council provides two main services to members—first, through its business house service. In June each year the Council sends albums with a selection of cards to over 600 large firms, for them to order, and arranges over-printing where necessary. Second, the Council sells its members' cards through retail outlets, the main one being the Royal Exchange, London, and other temporary shop premises in London and the provinces. (In 1973 the Council sold £130,000 worth of cards through its shops, of which one-third were sold through the Royal Exchange.) Whilst the Council believes that it helps to promote the sales of charity Christmas cards generally, through its press and media promotions, and will send out a charity's mail order catalogue on request, it admits that the levels of sales achieved through its outlets are of minor significance to the major card-selling charities. Each member charity selects six designs for the Council's shops, which have to be ready by May. If one design sells out then the charity can, with the approval of the Council, substitute another design. The cards must be cellophane wrapped, and can be sold singly or in packs, as the charity chooses. It is up to the individual charity to maintain a good level of stocks of its cards in the Council's shops.

The Council has an Advisory Committee which is made up of six people with experience in the field of charity Christmas cards sales. They will advise on designs and printers. This is a useful service, especially for the charity thinking of entering the field for the first time. To apply to the Council, a charity should write to The Secretary, Charity Christmas Card Council, 1 Longacre, London WC2. An invitation to attend the AGM held in April or May will be issued, and if it still wants to join, the charity then fills out the Council's application form.

Membership of the Council is not the panacea which some charities expect. The level of sales achieved through its shops is not high—it averages less than £200 per member; cellophane wrapping the cards and keeping the shops well stocked are both labour-intensive and may be beyond the capacities of some of the smaller charities. Delivery costs reduce profit margins as well, and can bring an ostensibly profitable operation perilously near failure.

The Council is only one of many schemes for the marketing of charity cards. It limits its membership to national charities—local charities may often find that the local council of social service in its area may organize similar schemes. The 1959 Committee is limited to twenty member charities, which have to be national, and concerned with the young, old or handicapped. A new member can be admitted only if one of the existing members resigns. It provides a marketing operation for its members' cards through temporary shops, similar to that offered by the Charity Christmas Card Council. Its turnover exceeds £100,000 a year, and an indication of its members' satisfaction is that only two or three have dropped out since 1959.

A consortium of charities combined to form Helpcards, to sell their cards to retailers, such as stores and shops. The operation cannot be said to be very profitable, as the size of the turnover is not yet sufficient to make up for the loss of the retailer's profit, which had hitherto accrued to the charity. Care Cards is the scheme of a card manufacturer, with some 25 per cent of the proceeds going to specified charities. Several major charities act as their own wholesalers, selling direct to stationers' and department stores. Some feel that charity Christmas cards should not be marketed through ordinary retail channels, because the profit margins possible bring so little benefit to the charity that they feel it is misleading to describe the cards as charity cards.

The choice of design will clearly affect the success of the charity's Christmas cards sales, whatever the popularity of the cause and the professionalism of the marketing, for an ugly card will not sell. There are various sources of designs. Art galleries and museums will usually, on application to the trustees, allow reproductions of exhibits to be sold by charities without any fee, or for a nominal amount. Some galleries produce the cards themselves and sell them to the charity at a discount; others may let the charity produce its own cards. A well-known artist may be prepared to design a card for a charity. In this case he should first be made aware of the need to keep production costs low, in case his design requires costly production techniques.

Charities can go to one of the large card manufacturers and choose cards from their range, which can be over-printed with the charity's name and, usually, the prefix, 'sold in aid of'; or bought more cheaply without over-printing. Two card manufacturers in particular have developed their 'charity service'—Webb Ivory and J. Arthur Dixon—and will also undertake the arduous task of distribution. The profit to the charity offered by these companies is usually 25 per cent of the value of sales. But charities going to card manufacturers should realize that they do not always have exclusive use of the design.

How does a charity decide on a design? Some prefer the card to reflect their image or advertise an aspect of their work, but the suitability of the cause varies. It is one thing to have a picture of an old building or a drawing of a child; quite another to have a sketch of a drug addict or a rehabilitated prisoner. Often the person selecting the design has no experience of what sells best, and has a taste too sophisticated for the mass market (often sentimental pictures of robins in the snow and little boys with donkeys sell best). The best-selling cards are noticeably undistinguished. If a charity is selecting a number of designs, then it is sensible to choose a range of styles, over a wide price range. For the charity expecting to sell a modest number of cards, it is more sensible to concentrate on the medium-to-high price range, since this raises the profit per unit sold and because they cannot hope to compete in price with those charities selling literally millions of cards, achieving low prices because of a huge print run.

A major problem for all charities which sell Christmas cards (and any other goods) is estimating the level of demand, to avoid over- or under-stocking. One advantage which commercial firms should offer is a topping-up service: the firm holds stocks of the cards, so if sales go better than estimated more supplies can be purchased at short notice. Thus the charity can buy cards without risking any capital, and its groups can order cards on a sale-or-return basis. The charity producing its own cards may under-estimate demand, and so lose both profits and good-will, through disappointing customers; or it may over-estimate demand and be left with unsold stocks. Past experience is clearly the best guide, but a charity entering the market for the first time would do well to ask the advice of the Charity Christmas Card Council Advisory Committee. The charity left with unsold stocks can try to sell them next year; can sell a variety of cards in bumper packs at reduced prices; or, if neither of these alternatives is available, can sell them off to retailers, generally at much reduced prices.

Trading

Over the past few years, several of the major card-selling charities have noticed a reduction in demand, as prices of postage and the cards themselves have risen. For many the level of money turnover has been maintained, because the cost of the cards has risen, but the number of cards sold has dropped or reached a plateau. Rising costs have squeezed the profitability of the operation still further, and many fear that the market is less buoyant than previously.

Gifts

The expansion of trading activities from cards to gifts was a logical step for charities and one which is likely to increase. Since they were establishing a marketing operation for cards, and especially when producing a mail order catalogue, it seemed sensible for charities to include a few items, like calendars and wrapping paper, which people could conveniently buy through the post, or through thrift shops, and at bazaars. From modest beginnings, many charities have developed very sophisticated mail order catalogues—the largest is that of Dr Barnardo's, which runs to nearly fifty pages and is supplemented by additional catalogues throughout the year.

Most charities concentrate on Christmas gifts, since the operation is usually very closely linked with the Christmas card operation. The range of goods varies from the specially designed items (such as Oxfam's dolls and games) to goods that can be purchased through normal retail shops (such as children's paint boxes or travelling chess sets).

Dealing in goods presents problems for charities. First, it is hard to know what to sell, especially where there has been no previous experience. Customers will have stronger feelings about the gifts they may buy from a charity than about the cards, apart from any other consideration because of the price. They may buy cards which are not 100 per cent to their taste, in order to support the charity, but are unlikely to be so magnanimous about gifts. Most charities try to overcome this problem by choosing goods that are already well tried, like the game of Monopoly, or by choosing goods so dull as to be inoffensive. Some charities, most notably Oxfam and the National Trust, strive for a recognizable 'house style' in their goods, which they see as an extension of their image; others are unconcerned, as long as the goods are not conspicuously bad value or shoddy.

Ballpoint pens or diaries or sticks of rock, marked with the charity's name, can all be sold, but are unlikely to yield much profit, as the quantities that have to be ordered to compete with such goods on the open market are usually so vast that the profit margins are low. How the goods will be sold affects the choice of what can be sold. If the bulk of the goods is likely to be sold in thrift shops, along with old clothes, then expensive, luxury items are inappropriate. If the goods are sold through the mail order catalogue, then it is important that the items should be easily packaged. Where the supporters of a charity are strongly motivated, and will sell goods to a wide circle of friends, then it is important to choose a sufficiently wide range of goods at suitable price.

How do charities in fact find suitable goods? If the charity wants to have original gifts, linked with its cause, or made by its beneficiaries, it should approach a well-known designer and ask him to produce a suitable design and to recommend a manufacturer. (To find a designer whose work would be suitable, look at similar goods on sale and ask the manufacturer for the name of the designer, or look at the goods at the Design Centre.) For the charity which wishes to play safe, there are two main sources of goods: one is to look at the items offered at Gift Fairs and the second is to use specialist wholesalers. The best known in the charity gift field is Webb Ivory Ltd. This firm offers goods on similar terms to its Christmas cards. Dealing with Webb Ivory has the advantage that the charity need hold no stock, and therefore has no capital outlay, and buys only when it has orders in hand. In fact, the National Society for the Mentally Handicapped Child operates the greater part of its £1 million card and gift operation through Webb Ivory Ltd, which even handles its orders and arranges the printing of its catalogues, so that the Society has a staff of only three people to deal with its trading. Webb Ivory usually offers 25 per cent profit margins on its goods to charity. Sometimes manufacturers will be especially helpful to charities, and may be prepared to consider selling to the charity on a sale-or-return basis, or at least hold stocks so that the charity need buy only once orders have been received.

Over-stocking is a real problem for charities. Left-over goods can be sold in thrift shops, or groups can be encouraged to sell items at bazaars and fêtes. But the profit margin on gifts is not high, the net profit rarely above 20 per cent—and any reduction in the margin, necessary to clear stocks, jeopardizes the whole profitability of the operation.

One aspect of trading which is not sufficiently exploited by charities, and which can offer much greater scope for large profit margins, is the special offer featured by newspapers or magazines. The media are often sympathetic and will feature one product, usually linked in some way to the cause, and often more expensive than the charity could normally expect to sell. This type of promotion is particularly suited to goods on which the mark-up is unusually high, and for which demand would be limited, rather than having the broad appeal which goods in a mail order catalogue must have. For example, War On Want was overwhelmed with orders for Coptic crosses featured in the *Sunday Times* on an Easter Sunday, which were in the £10–£45 price range. The charity which has suitably interesting, high priced goods should approach the Editor of the Woman's Page or the Features Editor (as appropriate) to seek support. If possible, it is best to carry few stocks, but to be able to obtain supplies quickly once orders are in hand.

Thrift shops

In the last decade the major charities have expanded their chains of thrift shops, so that these curious, permanent jumble sales have become a familiar sight in local high streets. Thrift shops, which usually stock mainly second-hand clothes, can be either temporary or permanent. For temporary shops the charity gets permission from the shop's owner to use an empty shop, until such time as it should be re-let. Usually the charity signs an undertaking to leave the premises on a week's or even a day's notice. The shop is provided rent free, or for a nominal rent, but the charity is liable for heat and light, and for rates. The premises and staff should be insured.

The most suitable premises for a thrift shop are in a busy area, with passing trade, though not necessarily in the main thoroughfare, and in a neighbourhood likely to attract suitable customers. Although a very posh area yields a plentiful supply of donated goods, both in quality and quantity, it is unlikely to attract the right customers. Goods can be collected and transported to the premises: customers cannot.

Once premises have been secured, the charity then has to find goods and staff. To find goods, a leaflet drop in the neighbourhood (or in any other neighbourhood) asking people to gather jumble (and preferably leaving plastic sacks and arranging to call back to collect the goods on a specific day in the near future) will usually yield a good supply. Once the shop is open, then people will bring gifts to the premises, and the process of attracting enough goods should take care of itself, and can be periodically boosted by further leaflet drops and by letters to the local press, reminding the public of the need for goods. Goods should be ruthlessly sorted; cleaned where necessary, discarded where useless (to a waste merchant) and offered for sale only when to do so would be consistent with the charity's good name.

Staffing a thrift shop is a major problem, and a good manageress can make all the difference between success and failure. Temporary shops are usually run by volunteer staff—either the charity's local group, or volunteers recruited from local organizations, often with the aid of the volunteer bureau of the local council of social services. Amongst the volunteers be sure to include someone able to collect and transport goods. As with all volunteers, there is a risk of unreliability, so try to ensure a large pool of helpers, in the event of some dropping out at short notice. The shop is, in the public mind, an extension of the charity, and its staff should be pleasant, helpful and cheerful—not the churlish crones sometimes found presiding over their jumble-like stock. The character of the manageress is most important, for her attitudes will permeate the rest of the helpers, and on her efficiency and honesty depends the profitability of the enterprise. She must be good at organizing volunteer helpers, able to price goods correctly, to keep the shop in good order and to keep rudimentary accounts. She may be unpaid, or paid a nominal wage.

If a temporary shop has been very successful in a particular area, and has built up a regular clientele and supply of goods, then it may be worth considering whether or not to make the venture permanent. Running a permanent thrift shop is harder than a temporary one, as effort has to be sustained; so volunteers may no longer be prepared to do the work, and there may be a need for paid staff; rent will have to be paid, except in the unlikely event of finding permanent, rent-free premises. The increased costs obviously reduce the profitability of the enterprise, and the charity should be wary, and consider establishing permanent shops only where a trial run (through a temporary shop) has shown the project is likely to succeed. Where a charity has established a number of permanent shops, it is usual to provide some supervision from headquarters, and also some new stock, such as Christmas cards and tea towels, to supplement the second-hand stock.

In assessing the value to the charity of its thrift shops, consideration also should be given to the publicity value of having the charity's name before large numbers of people who might otherwise be unaware of its existence. The shop can, of course, be a disadvantage in publicity terms—if it is dirty and tatty, and the goods over-priced and the staff unpleasant, then the charity's good name will be impugned.

There is nothing to stop a charity opening a shop that does not sell jumble but concentrates on new goods, or very high-class bric-a-brac and gifts. Few charities have done so because, for a charity to open up a shop on the same commercial lines as other retailers—that is, not relying on donated goods—involves much greater risk. Some charities do have shops selling specially produced goods (such as the National Trust and the Workshops for the Blind); others are very selective about the donated goods they will stock, consigning jumble to their thrift shops and putting all the choice pieces in one shop, in a suitably prosperous area. Dr Barnardo's Homes are about to launch a series of gift shops, to complement their catalogue trading, and absorb some left-over stock. It will be an experiment watched with interest by other charities. Some are considering opening shops to sell goods made by their beneficiaries, but are restrained by a reluctance to risk any capital. Certainly the expansion of charity shops is expected over the next decade.

Summary

Charities cannot trade as their primary object, but can do so through trading subsidiaries, which covenant their profits back to the parent body. The charity's tax liability on its trading activities is complex, especially with regard to VAT. Profits are made by charities over a wide range of trading, from Christmas cards to second-hand clothes. Thrift shops are an established method of fund-raising, requiring little outlay and risking no capital, or very little. Because profits are made by some, it does not mean that profits will be made by all, and competence and business flair are still the main ingredients for success.

9 Funds from central and local government

Grants from central and local government are of increasing importance to voluntary organizations as, more and more, the state assumes responsibility for services previously undertaken by charities. In fact, so marked has the trend become that many charities now plan to phase themselves out, having persuaded the government to assume responsibility for the service they are providing. (Whilst a charity cannot exert political pressure for the attainment of this end, the fact of its existence and its publicity could both contribute.)

Statutory funds, i.e. those from local or central government, are available to charities in a variety of ways. Where a voluntary organization is undertaking work for which the government department or local authority would otherwise be liable, then the voluntary organization will receive payment as of right. For example, a charity running an old people's home will receive a *per capita* payment for those without independent means. The availability of these grants which exist 'by right' should be known to those administering the charity. If there is uncertainty as to entitlement, then an enquiry can be made to the relevant government department or department of the local authority.

Grants which are made to voluntary organizations by government departments, at their discretion, total about £20 million a year. They may be made towards the running costs of the charity, because it is undertaking work of which the department approves and yet might not wish to undertake itself, as it lacks the necessary machinery. The government may want to see the work done on a temporary, experimental basis, and finds it easier to scrap a grant to a charity than to a government project. It is often cheaper for both local and central government to commission work from voluntary organizations rather than undertake the work itself: for example, research into homelessness is more easily done by a housing aid centre employing one extra person to monitor its case, than by setting up a separate research project.

Charities approaching government departments and local authorities for funds are often rather overawed by the machinery, and are anxious to arm themselves with seemingly impressive details as to what statute empowers the local or central government to give to its cause. Such information may be relevant to an appeal, as showing Parliament's general support for the work undertaken by the charity, but is not the cornerstone of an appeal, since it is the attitude of those applying the statute which will be crucial. Enormous discretionary powers are lodged with both government departments and local authorities, and as long as the charity is undertaking work for the public good it is usually possible for a grant to be made. As with other forms of funding, there are lean and fat times, but things would have to be very bad indeed for statutory funds to dry up completely.

Government departments

If you believe your charity is undertaking work for which the government may be prepared to make a grant, the first task is to consider which department is most likely to be receptive to the request. In most cases it is easy to determine which department is responsible for the field of work the charity undertakes. If it is not obvious, then the advice of the Voluntary Services Unit (see below, pp. 128–9) should be sought. Since government departments can be vast, it is important to find out whom to contact regarding a possible grant, as a misdirected application can take a long time to reach the right desk, if it ever does. The *Civil Service Year Book* (HMSO) lists senior civil servants in each department, with a summary of their responsibilities.

Even before making an informal approach, those applying on behalf of the charity must clarify in their own minds the grounds of their application, and what information will help their case. The civil servants with whom the charity will deal are not stupid, and have been trained to evaluate projects in a negative fashion, so a vague, half-worked-out enquiry is likely to meet with a sharp rebuff.

The information pertinent to an application is likely to be:

1. Some background information on the charity, e.g. when founded, with what aims, and how far and by what method these have been attained;
2. Scope of current work—whom it helps;
3. Proposal for future work, showing any expansion and the reason for it, and the support for such a project of those expert in the field;
4. Particular competence of the charity to undertake the work;
5. Reference to any legislation, or findings of any Royal Commission or Parliamentary Commission, which approves, in general terms, the work of the charity and emphasizes the value to the government of work in this field;
6. Saving to the government—showing costs to government if the work were not undertaken by the charity, either by having to provide the service itself, or because of the repercussions of the non-provision of the service, for example, on the social security payments, or emergency housing;
7. The financial position of the charity, and precise figures for expected expenditure and income in the next year. If the application is for a specific project, then accurate costings should be given. Do not be unrealistic in fixing the amount requested, either too high or too low: relate staff salaries to those in comparable fields (say, local government), and allow for overheads.

Once the charity has worked out the basis of its appeal, it must consider how best to make the approach. If the charity has an eminent trustee, likely to command the respect of those working in the field, then consider asking him to make an informal approach to the relevant civil servant (or minister, if the trustee is of sufficient eminence), to find out what form a formal application should take and what aspects of the work should be emphasized. Make sure that whoever makes the approach, however informally, is well briefed. It is useful for a charity, especially a little known one, to have an influential sponsor, because the civil servant will not be so quick to refuse an application out of hand, for fear of repercussions. Whoever makes the approach must try to win over the civil servant concerned, and should take care not to alienate him, or he will devote considerable energy to constructing a watertight case for refusal.

All departments have their own criteria for judging the worth of voluntary organizations' projects. Some will only support projects which further departmental objectives; others will support unpopular projects which would otherwise close down; and others will only encourage innovations. Some try to do all three things simultaneously. Some departments have greater flexibility in giving to voluntary organizations than others, related to their budgeting. Some departments specifically allow for small grants to be made; others limit themselves to research funds and will not consider applications for running costs. This information is necessary for a charity so it can frame its application correctly. It is no good trying to dress up a project to fit into a department's favoured form, but for example, if a department has funds only for research, then a project can be described as action research, and provision made for monitoring the charity's work.

If a department is sympathetic to the charity's work but cannot make a grant at that particular time, then the charity must be careful not to force the department into a categorical refusal, but to leave the rejection vague, so that a future application can be made.

If a government department rejects a charity's requests for funds for no apparent good reason, then it is open to the charity to take the matter further and to resort to political pressure. This is a weapon which should be used with care—it is likely to alienate the civil servant concerned and turn him into an enemy. (However, if he acts like one anyhow, there is nothing to be lost.) There are a number of people on whom pressure can be put. First, one can complain to the boss of the civil servant concerned (he will be listed in the *Civil Service Year Book*). It helps if the complaint comes from someone eminent. If this yields no satisfactory reply, then complain to the minister. If he is unhelpful, then ask an MP to raise the matter at parliamentary question time. (To find a sympathetic MP, approach either the local MP or one known to be interested in the charity's cause—Vacher's *Parliamentary Companion* lists MPs and their addresses.) Depending on how acrimonious the exchange becomes, the charity can use publicity to advertise its grievance against the department.

The Voluntary Services Unit (Home Office)

The VSU is a fairly recent creation, with a four-fold aim:

1. To be a friend to voluntary organizations within Whitehall, helping them find their way around central government departments;
2. It acts as an informal co-ordinator of government support for voluntary organizations. Each government department has a VSU liaison officer and they meet quarterly to discuss issues affecting the voluntary sector *vis-à-vis* their departments;
3. It stimulates the use of community volunteers (largely by substantial grants to the Volunteer Centre and Young Volunteer Force Foundation);
4. It acts as a financier of last resort.

A voluntary organization hoping to secure a grant from a government department can receive advice from the VSU as to whom to approach in the department, what funds the department is likely to have, and possibly even advice on how to frame the appeal. The VSU should be taken at its word, and used as a friend and counsellor to voluntary organizations. If a government department is unhelpful, then it is sensible to solicit the help of the VSU to find out why. It will not be able to override a department's decision, or fund a project where another department has the responsibility and authority to do so, but has decided not to.

The VSU has a budget of under £2 million a year. It makes grants to voluntary organizations, or their projects, where no clear departmental responsibility exists and/or the work spans the interest of more than one government department. It regards itself as a financier of last resort. Most grants are made to national organizations, but local projects can be funded where they are of national significance. The Unit does not have 'a programme', and fund projects which fall within it, but rather funds a variety of projects and organizations, which it considers worthwhile – in its own words, 'acting as a safety net for organizations which could not otherwise be accommodated within Whitehall'. In view of the strict limitation of government resources, the Unit has established the following priorities: first, to meet existing commitments; second, to assist projects which are threatened with bankruptcy but whose work is of high social priority; and last, only then, to undertake the funding of new projects. The Unit is noted for the flexibility of its approach and, in Whitehall's terms, the speed of its response.

To apply for funds from the Unit, first, make an informal approach, roughly outlining the problem. (Note the points relevant to an appeal for government funds, above, p. 126.) Seek guidance on how best to frame the application. The VSU will want to know why the charity believes it falls within its frame of reference, and what attempts have been made to secure financial support elsewhere. Charities may expect a helpful attitude from the VSU, 'their friend in Whitehall'. If the VSU cannot help the charity financially, then ask for guidance on where else the charity may seek funds. To some extent VSU funding will depend, as all government funding, on the economic situation and the attitude of the government of the day to the funding of the voluntary sector, for, like all government departments, its income is, in the last resort, determined by Parliament.

The Urban Programme

Under the co-ordinating umbrella of the Home Office, the government disburses over £15 million a year to areas of special social need (with the local authorities' contribution, the Urban Programme totals £21 million per annum). The money is channelled to local authorities, who may undertake the work themselves or sponsor voluntary organizations' projects. The local authority must meet 25 per cent of the cost of the projects in their area, and the Urban Programme will pay the remaining 75 per cent. Where the local authority sponsors a voluntary organization's application, it signifies its preparedness to pay that organization 25 per cent of the cost. Applications can only be made by a local authority, and in some cases a charity may find difficulty in finding a local authority to sponsor its application, since it involves the local authority in 25 per cent of the cost and it may be for work it is not anxious to support. Not all local authorities seek grants under the Urban Programme, except as a way of defraying their own costs by limiting applications to their own projects—although the government circular specifically asks local authorities to encourage participation of voluntary organizations in the Urban Programme. One unfortunate aspect of the way the Urban Programme works is that the worst authorities, i.e. those that offer the least amount of social services which they can possibly get away with, are likely to be the least anxious to sponsor voluntary organizations' applications for Urban Programme funds, since they have to pay 25 per cent of the cost. Even where charities can find a sponsoring local authority, it does not ensure success, since applications for grants exceed the supply of funds by five to one.

Urban Programme grants are limited to urban areas of 'special social need'. The term has been left deliberately vague, so that flexibility can be exercised in making grants. As a rough guide, the Home Office provides this definition:

> Areas of special social need mean areas within towns and cities containing those who are relatively deprived by national standards and where pressure on social services is severe. Evidence of social need may take many forms – poverty, high levels of unemployment, over-crowding, lack of basic household amenities, old and dilapidated housing, educational disadvantage, inadequate community service, a poor quality environment. Many such areas have substantial ethnic minorities.

The Urban Programme aims to provide additional funds for local authorities which have particularly great needs.

Each year the Home Office issues a circular inviting applications for grants under the Urban Programme. This lays out the main areas of interest for which grants will be considered, as well as giving details of the manner and form of application. (Charities wishing to apply for grants should ask for a copy of the latest circular from the Home Office, Urban Programme, Horseferry House, Dean Ryle Street, London SW1.) The range of projects which are eligible for grants is very wide, and those helped in the past include day nurseries, language classes for immigrants, housing aid centres, lunch clubs for the elderly, family planning and legal advice centres. Projects which will have a reasonably rapid effect are favoured.

Grants are usually made for a period up to five years (renewable for a further five-year period if special social need continues to exist). Grants may also be made for capital projects; generally these must be for less than £100,000. Clearly, the Urban Programme has to spread its resources widely, so favours small-scale projects. For grants for capital projects, the Urban Programme will normally consider funding both capital costs and the running costs for five years.

As has been said before, all grants are submitted by local authorities, whether for their own projects, undertaken by their staff, or for projects run by voluntary organizations within their areas. The local authority must place all its proposals in order of priority, as a guide to the Home Office. Usually the local authority's preferences will be noted, but an inexpensive project of low priority may be approved, whereas a costly project of higher priority may be rejected. Local authorities are not obliged to submit for consideration all proposals voluntary organizations put forward—they can do so or not, at their discretion. Because the support of the local authority is crucial in securing grants from the Urban Programme, both as a sponsor and for giving the project high priority, it is worth while enlisting the support of the relevant people in the local authority (see below, p. 132).

The form of application for grants from the Urban Programme is very specific. A proposal should not normally exceed six pages, including the financial statement. It should include the following information.

1. Name of project, and of the organization undertaking it;
2. Information on the area, and its population, including brief description of its needs;
3. Description of the project and its aims;
4. Description of any arrangements for monitoring the progress of the projects;
5. A summary of the views of local organizations and residents (if they have been consulted);
6. Number and type of staff to be employed, with salary scales;
7. Estimated date when the project will start operating;
8. For buildings—area of accommodation to be provided; type of construction; estimated starting and completion dates; whether it provides access for the disabled;
9. Financial statement—to follow a prescribed form (forms obtainable from the Home Office).

Applications to the Urban Programme involve a local authority in a great deal of work—making sure that applications are made in the right form, deciding on which projects to submit, and in what order of priority. Charities are well advised to consider applications for the Urban Programme well in advance, as the local authority may require three or four months to process applications and steer them through the necessary council committees. It is no good a charity noting that applications have to be at the Home Office by 31 October, and submitting theirs to the local authority on 1 October: by then it is likely to be too late. If there is any chance that your charity may qualify for a grant under the Urban Programme, then contact the local authority and ask for a copy of the next government circular on the Urban Programme, and ask when applications should be received by the local authority.

Local authorities

Government departments vary considerably in their attitudes towards funding voluntary organizations, but local authorities are even less predictable. The main reason is that local authorities may give to voluntary organizations under discretionary powers, and each council interprets these powers differently. Not only can the local authority disburse funds to voluntary organizations, it is also critical in securing grants under the Urban Programme. Also, the local authorities may waive the rates due on a charity's premises: 50 per cent relief is automatically granted; the other 50 per cent can be waived at the discretion of the local authority. It may also let a charity use short-life accommodation, and provide a myriad of other valuable services.

It is important to know where the power lies in dealing with a local authority, so that the right allies can be sought, to support an application for funds. Councils of elected members usually delegate their powers to committees, the full council retaining the right to ratify or reject committee decisions. Each committee has a chairman who has considerable power, not only as leader of the majority group on the committee but also because it is he who will make decisions that need to be taken in between committee meetings. He and the committee work closely with their chief officials. The balance of power between the committee, the committee chairman and the chief officer depends on their respective personalities. A chief officer who alienates his committee chairman and the committee in general is quite likely to be removed. A charity hoping to secure funds from a local authority should attempt to secure the backing of the committee chairman and the chief officer. (A list of local authority committees, their chairmen and chief officers can be found in the *Municipal Year Book*.) Ask your trustees if they know the relevant people, or judge whether they would command their respect. If your trustees are not likely to enhance an appeal, then try to find someone who would. All the benefits of having a prestigious sponsor are pertinent to an appeal to a local authority.

When framing a formal application, cover the same points as to a government department (see above, p. 126) and add specific information on the benefit to the residents of the area. Relate the project to local need, and if possible point to real savings to the local authority. For example, a housing aid centre, by preventing homelessness, will save the local authority the exceptionally high cost of temporary accommodation; or a day centre for old people will lessen the burden to the social services department.

The tone of the appeal is important. Whatever their politics, local councillors are likely to be staid members of the community. This must be taken into account when drafting the appeal.

If a local authority is adamant in refusing support, then a charity can use political pressure. Appeal may be made to the opposition group on the council (this may just harden the opposition of the majority group), or to a local councillor of the ruling group to raise the issue in Council. A very effective way to gain backing for one's case, and force the local authority to back down, is to enlist the help of the local press. This will, at least, force the council to look at an application very seriously before rejecting it.

Funds from the EEC

Since Britain's entry into the Common Market, UK charities have become increasingly hopeful of receiving grants from Community funds. The EEC is seen as having limitless funds available to those who can cut through the red tape to get at them. In fact, very little has yet become available, although it is expected that as the EEC develops and its area of interest widens more funds will be available to the voluntary sector.

Two schemes for funding voluntary organizations have so far been established, the European Social Fund and the Poverty Programme.

The European Social Fund is, despite its title, in effect an employment and training fund, designed to facilitate the integration of migrant workers and their families. Grants from the Social Fund have to be matched by grants from the UK government. The amount available from the Fund is considerable—over £25 million a year.

Applications, which have to follow a prescribed format, must be made through the Department of Employment. In fact, although voluntary organizations can apply for a grant from the Social Fund, government policy has been to discourage such applications, and instead apply to the Social Fund for reimbursement of 50 per cent of the cost of projects which it has already funded. Thus the UK government uses the European Social Fund to recover some of its grants to voluntary organizations. One reason for this, apart from the government's parsimony, is that payment from the Social Fund is so slow (around eighteen months) that only the government has the resources to run a project for eighteen months before getting funds. In view of the way in which the government uses the Social Fund, perhaps a charity's best hope of getting some of the money is to suggest to the Department of Employment when seeking a government grant that the Department defray 50 per cent of the cost by applying to the Social Fund on the charity's behalf. (About half the Department's applications to the Social Fund have been successful.)

The European Poverty Programme is one of the short-term programmes which the EEC devises from time to time, under which voluntary organizations may qualify for grants. The Poverty Programme is initially for two years (1976–8) and will make available £200,000 for action research projects in the UK. This amount has to be matched by government grants. Applications were channelled through the DHSS who, in fact, chose from projects submitted to it from a working party of the National Council of Social Service, though not fully accepting its recommendations. (The money will be made available for community groups and resource centres.)

To keep informed on possible sources of funds from the EEC budget, and community decisions in the social welfare field, charities should read *Look Europe*, published eleven times a year by the NCSS.

Summary

Statutory funds, whether from local or central government, are becoming of increasing importance to charities. Grants may be made by government departments, by the Voluntary Services Unit, through the Urban Programme or by local authorities. A limited amount of money is available from the EEC.

To secure statutory funds, a charity should ascertain first, if it is eligible, what type of information will be needed to support its application. It should try to establish friendly contacts with the civil servants and politicians involved, whether in local or central government. If a government department or local authority appears to be rejecting an application unreasonably, then a charity can try to bring political pressure to bear, and back up its case with publicity.

10 Mobilizing other groups

Over 8,000 British and Irish organizations are listed in the *Directory of British Associations*, and its authors estimate that there are more than a quarter of a million clubs and associations in the UK. In many cases these groups provide a rich source of funds for charities, either through joint fund-raising efforts or because the groups are made up of well-to-do and charitably disposed members. The range of groups is enormous, and clearly each charity will find certain groups more sympathetic to its cause than others.

Groups can be invited to join in a charity's general fund-raising campaigns, for example, providing flag sellers or house-to-house collectors, or can be asked to participate in a tailor-made campaign, reflecting joint interests. Before approaching them, be clear as to what you would like them to do. Try to find out something about the way in which the group works, and note any joint schemes with charities in the past. It is very useful when approaching a group to be able to propose a scheme which has a time limit—perhaps a year, or over the Christmas or Easter periods—as people are reluctant to undertake open-ended commitments. Be sure to have interesting literature on your charity's work, which will help to show its worth and, if possible, arrange for some leading light in the group, or its national committee, to see something of the charity's work at first hand.

Ideally, the group will adopt the charity as its cause of the year and organize a fund-raising campaign on its behalf, with the charity's involvement limited to providing information on its work and collecting the cheque at the end. Often a group will not be prepared to be so totally committed, and will go little beyond sending out general literature on behalf of the charity with its own mailings. This can be useful to the charity, for it is a way of reaching a large number of people at minimal cost—for example, the Automobile Association has a membership of over four million people. The material sent can be a general leaflet, or may be specifically designed—if the likely response merits a special leaflet. Sometimes the material will be included free of charge; on other occasions the charity bears any additional postal costs.

Sometimes certain groups are useful allies in campaigning, and a statement supporting the charity's aims, say, from the president, can be of great value, adding a stamp of respectability. Similarly, professional groups may, through willing members, provide free, otherwise expensive services.

To find groups likely to be most sympathetic, consult two invaluable directories, both generally available in public libraries. The first is the *Directory of British Associations* (CBD Research Ltd, 154 High Street, Beckenham, Kent). This lists over 8,000 associations in the UK and Ireland, giving their membership figures, publications, activities and interests. The second directory, *Current British Directories*, lists 2,500 directories published in the UK, Ireland, the Commonwealth and South Africa, and is useful because it includes the handbooks of associations and groups, many of which give the names and addresses of members.

Church groups

Churches are ideal for charity fund-raising, as they have a large overall membership, a national organization and are committed to the virtues of charity. Some causes are clearly more likely to attract church support than others, for example, the building funds of famous churches or cathedrals, missionary activities or social work directed by clerics, and therefore assured of having Christian content. Often various church groups feel themselves allied to specific denominational charities, such as Christian Aid or CAFOD, and the national leadership will be reluctant to sponsor the appeal of what they may regard as a rival charity. The best way to avoid a refusal is to have a church leader ask his colleagues on your charity's behalf. It may take several attempts to find a willing bishop, but it is worth the effort. If the national leadership of the church concerned refuses to sponsor an appeal, despite the fact that a leading churchman is supporting the request, then consider whether the appeal could go out to member churches directly, sponsored simply by the friendly bishop. Before undertaking the cost of a mailing to all churches, or those within one denomination, consider if the likely return warrants the expense. It might be better to limit the appeal to churches within a certain area. Another way of reaching the member churches without the expense of a mass mailing is to secure the support of a leading churchman and hold a launching event designed to gain publicity. For example, a newspaper report of Bishop X appealing for support for your charity, asking churches to hold collections, should produce some response. This can be backed by advertising in the church press.

One of the problems of launching an appeal to churches is that the number of churches is large, so mailing costs are high, and the churches receive many requests for help—most from neighbourhood causes which they feel most obliged to support. Appeals from national charities are, therefore, quite likely to be rejected; although if the appeal is repeated year after year the church may be increasingly reluctant to turn it down. So if there are sufficient funds to sustain repeated appeals to church groups, then the results may be increasingly rewarding.

To contact the various church groups, use the relevant directories. (Listed here are the ones for the principal church and religious groups; others may be found in the *Current British Directories*.)

The Church of England: The *Church of England Year Book*—the official yearbook of the General Synod (Church Information Office, Church House, Dean's Yard, London SW1) lists the dioceses of the Church of England, bishops, etc., and from this one can write to each diocese for the Official Yearbook and Clergy list, published by each diocesan Board of Finance, which lists churches and ministers in the area.

The Church of Ireland: The *Church of Ireland Directory* (Irish Publications, 59 Merrion Square, Dublin 2) lists clergy, parishes, etc.

The Church of Scotland: Church of Scotland Year Book (Church of Scotland, 121 George Street, Edinburgh) lists parishes, arranged by synods and presbyteries.

The Roman Catholic Church: The *Catholic Directory* (Search Press, 85 Gloucester Road, London SW7) lists parishes, priests and clergy. The *Catholic Directory for Scotland* (John S. Burns, 25 Finlay Street, Glasgow) gives the same information for Scotland. *Irish Catholic Directory* (James Duffy & Co., 21 Shaw Street, Dublin) lists Roman Catholic churches and clergy in Ireland.

Baptists: Baptist Handbook (Council of Baptist Union of Great Britain and Ireland) lists churches and pastors.

Methodists: Methodist Church Directory (Methodist Publishing House, 2 Chester House, Pages Lane, London N10) lists ministers and churches.

United Reformed Church: Handbook of the United Reformed Church (no publisher yet announced) lists congregational and presbyterian churches in England and Wales. *Congregational Union of Scotland Year Book* (CUS, 217 West George Street, Glasgow) lists congregational churches in Scotland.

Scottish Episcopal Church: Scottish Episcopal Church Yearbook & Directory (Representative Church Council, 21 Grosvenor Crescent, Edinburgh) lists parishes and ministers.

Free Church: Free Church Council: Annual Report & Directory (27 Tavistock Square, London WC1) lists federations and councils. *Free Church of Scotland Year Book* (Knox Press, 15 North Bank Street, Edinburgh) lists churches and ministers.

Unitarians: Unitarian & Free Churches Directory (General Assembly, 1–6 Essex Street, Strand, London WC2) lists congregations and ministers.

Quakers: Religious Society of Friends (Friends Book Centre, Friends House, Euston Road, London NW1) lists meetings.

Jews: Jewish Year Book (Jewish Chronicle Publications, 67 Great Russell Street, London WC1) includes lists of synagogues.

Professional groups

Certain professions may seem likely to be sympathetic to certain charities—for example, doctors to medical training, architects to the preservation of historic buildings, surveyors to housing projects. Appropriate groups may be found in the *Directory of British Associations*, and lists of members can often be found via *Current British Directories*, for example, for doctors, lawyers, accountants, architects and surveyors. Sometimes the national body of these groups mails its members regularly and will include a charity's appeal with the mailing. It is best if the appeal is signed by a prominent member of the profession. It may be possible to interest the group in adopting a project, and assuming financial responsibility for it, perhaps thus gaining the right to name the project—for example, after a past president. In some cases professional bodies will have a charitable cause each year; in others little more is done beyond drawing members' attention to a worthy cause.

The advantages of directing an appeal to a professional group are that its members are usually relatively affluent, so can afford to give, and, second, the cause can be linked to the known interests of the group. For example, a successful appeal to stockbrokers, on behalf of an overseas aid charity, started 'Will you invest in the future of the Third World?'

Philanthropic organizations

Some organizations, such as Rotary Clubs, Lions, Round Table, Soroptimists and Freemasons, have philanthropy as part of their aims. It is invaluable to a charity to win the support of these bodies, for once they have assumed the commitment they will raise funds independently, and usually give substantially.

The national bodies of such organizations do not like to sponsor appeals, as their organizations are supposedly not fund-raising, though constituent groups do in fact raise funds. To persuade a group to raise funds for a specific charity, contact the local secretary (the Town Hall will normally be able to supply his name and address) and ask if the group would be interested in having a speaker from the charity, to talk on its work, and its need for help. It might be useful to national organizers of the charity to have a list of, for example, Rotary clubs throughout the country.

Such lists do, in fact, exist, but they are usually issued only to members.

The London livery companies disburse funds to charity, and can be regarded as philanthropic organizations, or as trusts—some are listed in the *Directory of Grant-Making Trusts.* A complete list of livery companies can be found in the *City of London Directory* (City Press). Applications to them may be by letter, with support material, or, in the first instance, by a personal approach. Each has its own criteria for giving, and it is useful for the charity to build up this information for future reference. The livery companies, as City institutions, respond best to City appeals, especially those sponsored by the Lord Mayor or past Lord Mayors.

Trade unions

Both the Trade Union Congress and individual unions make donations to charities. A wide range of causes is supported—everything from a convalescent home to aid to refugees from totalitarian régimes.

Applications to the TUC are considered by the Finance Committee, which recommends to the Council which charities should receive support. Although the TUC is anxious not to be inundated with requests, it is hard to see how a charity could expect to receive a grant, at least where it has not done so previously, without applying. So in order to be considered, charities should write to the Finance Committee. Similarly, in individual unions recommendations on which charities to support are made by their Finance Committees to their Executives. Applications should be made to the Finance Committee. (A list of trade unions, with the names and addresses of their secretaries, is to be found in the list of delegates, published annually by the Trade Union Congress.)

Mention should also be made of the 'penny a week' schemes which operate in some factories, whereby employees agree to have a small contribution to charity docked from their pay. Such schemes require a substantial amount of organization and the co-operation of the employer, whose wages clerks assume the responsibility for collecting the money. Generally, such schemes have to be done on a large scale before the costs of organizing them are recouped. 'Penny a week' schemes share the advantage of banker's orders: once people have agreed to participate they stay in the scheme—largely through inertia.

Local groups

When launching a local appeal, it is useful to try to involve as many local groups as possible. Local scouts groups can be asked to deliver leaflets door-to-door; local choirs to carol sing; local churches can be asked to hold special services; political parties to send collectors for flag days; women's groups to knit blankets or help in a temporary thrift shop. It is important to try to involve as many groups as possible. An appeal in the local paper should be backed up by letters to the secretary of each group. (A list of the groups in the area is usually available from the town hall.)

Often local groups will be involved in their own fund-raising programmes; but they may help, especially for a local cause, on a one-off basis. Approaches to local organizations can be made either by the charity's own local group or, in the absence of one, by the charity's headquarters.

Special interest groups

Certain aspects of a charity's work may be of interest to specific groups. For example, the British Co-operative movement supported an Oxfam project to establish co-operatives in Botswana, and women's groups will often support charities to benefit women, such as cancer control clinics or women's literacy campaigns. It might not be the cause which is of joint interest—it might be the method of raising the money: for example, Friends of the Earth might be prepared to help with re-cycling schemes; choral societies may give a carol concert. Some ingenuity is needed to match the groups and the projects.

Sometimes groups approach a charity with proposals for a joint programme. Care must be taken to see that offers of help are financially viable. Sometimes a group will offer its services in good faith, yet the charity will end up covering their losses—for example, for the school drama group which wants to stage a play in a 2,000-seat theatre; or the amateur orchestra which wants to stage a grandiose concert. Remember, it is better to refuse an offer of help, and risk alienating some support, than to lose substantial amounts of money and incur the blame for the failure. Consider how groups can be useful to the charity, not how your charity can be useful to the group. One of the first lessons a good fund-raiser has to learn is to say no to all the daft proposals that he will receive, purportedly to benefit his cause.

Summary

Groups such as churches, trade unions, professional associations and clubs provide a framework which can be used by charities to reach hundreds of thousands of people. If a charity is to succeed in mobilizing these groups, it must devise a campaign based either on the relevance of the cause or on the relevance of the method of raising money. Local groups should always be asked to help with local campaigns.

Approaches to organizations will be more successful if endorsed by a leading member of the group. This is true whether the approach is to a church, a livery company or the local branch of the Anglers' Association. Some organizations, such as churches, are predisposed to charitable work, and this can be emphasized when making the approach. Often groups are in need of funds themselves, and will welcome the suggestion of a joint fund-raising effort. Take care not to allow any organization to involve the charity in hare-brained fund-raising projects.

11 Publicity and advertising

Why publicity is needed

A charity that is unknown to the public, or at least to that section of it from which it hopes to attract funds, is unlikely to be successful. A charity's publicity should aim to:

1. Establish the charity's credentials (usually through the association of well-known and well respected individuals);
2. Make it known to those from whom it hopes to secure funds;
3. Gain sympathy and understanding for its cause and press for an alleviation of the conditions creating the need for its existence;
4. Show that giving money to it can ameliorate suffering.

Some causes are better known and understood than others and need little explanation as to their basic purpose, which may be implicit in their names—for example, the Cancer Research Fund or Help The Aged. Others are unknown, or their cause not really understood, so the public needs information on them before they can be expected to give.

Whilst knowing what a charity does is a prerequisite, it will not necessarily stimulate a donation. Publicity must overcome the natural resistance to give. It must present the charity as a worthwhile cause. Most people feel more generally drawn to some causes than others—for example, children and medical research are highly regarded, others, such as drug addicts and unmarried mothers, are thought of as undeserving, having 'brought it on themselves'. Publicity must educate the public to a more sympathetic and considered reaction, making the apparently undeserving seem deserving. It must counteract existing prejudices about the charity's cause—for example, that the homeless are feckless, or alcoholics merely weak-willed. Showing children as beneficiaries is a usual way of trying to popularize one's cause: thus a community for the mentally retarded will refer to its inmates as 'children', though their ages may run from ten to forty-five. This tries to make one's cause more attractive, but must be used within reason and not become window dressing rather than education, lest it be regarded as somewhat dishonest. Sometimes charities will try to exploit prejudices to benefit their own particular cause—for example, Dr Barnardo's Homes with the plaint 'Shouldn't charity begin at home . . .'—but most charities eschew such publicity, as likely to backfire to the detriment of all charities.

A charity's publicity must not only identify an area of need and stimulate sympathy for its cause: it must also show that money can help the problem. It is helpful to tell prospective donors how their money is likely to be spent, either by reference to how it was spent in the past ('The crop yield of this village in Africa has increased tenfold since we brought irrigation to the area'), or by showing what it could achieve in the future ('£365 will house a family'). This brings people a feeling that money can help the problem, even if it cannot solve it. Be sure in all publicity to adopt this hopeful attitude, or else potential donors will feel that there is nothing that can be done and throw up their hands in despair—an action which benefits no one. Another aspect of projecting a hopeful, successful attitude is that people like to identify themselves with successful enterprises. If a charity is seen as lively, optimistic and really achieving great goals, it is more likely to secure support than a charity which projects gloom and failure, a donation to which would seem to be throwing good money after bad. A charity must never gloss over the problems it seeks to resolve, or underestimate the difficulty of its task; but it should show that it can provide at least some of the answers, and a solution if enough funds were available.

An important aspect of any charity's work is the educational and campaigning function it fulfils. Nowadays it is not regarded as sufficient for a charity to distribute alms without trying to solve the underlying causes which produce the need for aid. Of course, this can rarely be done with complete success, but it is regarded as proper for a modern charity to give priority to changing the basic situation, rather than simply offering palliatives. For example, the

K

Spastics Society, not generally regarded as a campaigning or radical charity, tries to overcome the causes of the problems of spasticity by sponsoring research, as well as devoting funds to helping spastics. War on Want, through its educational work in this country, aims at creating better trading relations with the developing countries, which would have a more profound effect in promoting the prosperity of these countries than the £1 million a year that War on Want might send in alms. It is through its publicity that a charity's educational, campaigning work is carried out. It must also be remembered that if a charity can successfully mobilize public opinion to force government action, it is likely to release funds far greater than it would be able to secure by itself. And it has been argued very persuasively that charities should devote their resources to this type of pressure group activity rather than dishing out funds, and that they would have disproportionately great effect if they did so. (This type of view makes the Charity Commissioners nervous, but in fact there would seem quite a lot of leeway in the charity laws to allow this type of pressure group activity—witness the Child Poverty Action Group.)

Ideally in one's publicity, one seeks to identify one's charity with its cause; thus housing = Shelter, overseas aid = Oxfam. In fact, there are many charities that deal with housing and overseas aid; but these two charities have, through successful publicity, secured the prime role in the public mind. This supremacy in the field (known in the commercial world as 'brand leadership') has great financial spin-off, in securing indirectly solicited gifts, such as legacies. This identification of one's charity with the cause is ideal, but not always possible. For one thing, there are often a multiplicity of organizations working in the same field. In that case, a charity should try in its publicity to show what distinguishes it from the others. (If nothing distinguishes it from all other charities in the field, then serious consideration should be given to amalgamation.)

The amount one can afford to spend on publicity is linked to considerations of the likely returns. Spending on publicity does not simply mean advertising; it means devoting people's time and energy to getting the charity better known—time that could be spent on other activities. Also, it should be noted that charities find paid publicity (i.e. advertising) rarely covers its cost. One must strive for the level of publicity appropriate to one's needs. If appealing for £20,000 for a counselling service for teenagers, then advertising in the national press at £4,000 a page is not sensible; conversely, if launching an appeal for £500,000, it is sensible to include in the budget some funds for publicity. This does not necessarily mean spending money on advertising: in the first instance it means devoting human resources to the task of winning publicity.

So that the charity may avoid damaging its cause by appearing hypocritical, care must be taken to ensure that its publicity is in keeping with the spirit of the campaign. For example, a stupid, unthinking attempt to gain publicity which reverberated badly on the organization was the motor cavalcade organized by an anti-motorway group. Similarly, a lavish banquet in aid of War on Want or Oxfam would be inappropriate and would cause adverse publicity. Apart from avoiding certain types of activities because they would be in bad taste, and would cause bad publicity, be careful that your charity does not speak with a cleft tongue, projecting one image to donors and another to those it seeks to help. That is the sort of situation that can be guaranteed to cause internal dissension in the charity, and provide the sort of adverse publicity that always seems to secure press coverage!

Types of publicity and how to get them

Press coverage

Press coverage falls into two main categories: that which one pays to secure (advertising) and editorial coverage. The advantage of advertising is that one can control the content, but it is extremely expensive. Editorial coverage has the advantage of being free, and also it is more generally read than the advertising columns, and almost certainly treated as more reliable. The main ways of gaining editorial coverage for a charity's work or fund-raising events are by press releases (written or spoken), press conferences and organizing stunts for the press.

The press falls into distinctive categories—local, national and specialist. The main differences are obvious, but one should bear in mind that local papers are more anxious for one's news story, and also that they generally have more time, if publishing weekly, and so one has more leeway on deadlines. But the cardinal rule in dealing with the press should be observed in the cases of both the national and local press—

Always be reliable, and make sure you give the correct facts.
Do not trouble the press with trivia, or you will lose credibility as a worthwhile source.

Editorial coverage: If your charity has a local (or specialist) paper on which it is hoped to secure regular coverage, then try to build up a relationship with a reporter on the paper. This is not as difficult as it sounds—simply phone up and introduce yourself as the person now dealing with publicity for your charity; try to establish a social relationship; but do not pester any reporter—think of the possible consequences of his petulance! Read the paper yourself, so that you can appreciate the type of story they like.

If you think you have a story of national significance, then send the story to the national press. Remember, the national press is not homogeneous: there are great differences between the popular and quality press, both in the news they cover and their treatment of it. A great deal of wasted effort can be spared if a basic grasp of these differences is mastered before attempting publicity. Remember, if you trouble the press needlessly you will be regarded in much the same light as the boy who cried 'wolf'. A general point worth noting is that Sunday papers will give more feature articles than news stories.

Press release: Stories and information sent to the press should be factual. Avoid flowery language, and do not try to pad it out. The journalists are there to impose the style on your information! If the release is about an event make sure that you include all relevant information—where, when, how much and type of event—and, in all press releases, why it is being done. It is a good ploy to include a quotation from the head of the charity about the cause, as quotations are picked up by the press: they help to personalize a report. Local newspapers are more likely to print a press release as you send it; national newspapers can be depended on to re-hash a release. Always send press releases on headed paper, which includes the name and address of the organization. It should be typed, with double spacing and wide margins (to allow the sub-editors space to mark the copy). Type on one side of the paper only. Always date it, and give the name and phone number (day and evening) of a person to contact for further information (this is crucial). If sending a photograph, make sure it is captioned, describing the action or naming the people, and giving the charity's name and address and name and phone number of the person to contact. Stick the caption on the back of the photograph—do not write on it!

Before sending off press releases, telephone the newspaper and find out whom they like the stories sent to—usually the Editor or the News Editor. Send a copy to him and also to any contact you may have on the paper. Always send two copies, as your contact may be away, and if you send a copy to the Editor or News Editor you can be confident that someone will be assuming that role. Find out when the paper goes to press, and make sure your press release arrives in good time. If trying to get advance publicity for a specific event, use common sense and do not send the advance press release six months ahead of time—it will get lost; a month is usually ample notice. If the event might yield an interesting photograph, then mention this in your advance press release, so that the newspaper knows to send a photographer along.

When you have good reason, telephone the national press; that is, when you have newsworthy information that needs relaying quickly. Remember that journalists are busy people, with evening deadlines. There is no point in approaching them late in the day, except for very, very important stories. When telephoning, unless you have a contact ask for the News Desk or, if it is a picture story, for the Picture Desk. Be clear in your own mind as to what you are going to say before you pick up the telephone.

The names and addresses of all national and local newspapers, trade, technical and specialist magazines and journals, are listed in the *PR Planner* (Media Information Ltd). It also lists the names of correspondents on the various papers.

The quickest way of sending out any news story is through the Press Association. You can telephone a story through their copy desk and they will, at their discretion, pass it on to the appropriate media (this includes television, radio and the press). It will only be interested in a story that has some national significance. A number of large charities subscribe to Universal News Services. In return for an annual subscription the UNS relays any stories sent to them over a teleprinter. This is of advantage if a large number of stories are placed, particularly at short notice.

Press conferences: these should be held only if the news is sufficiently important to justify the journalists' time. (They will not thank you for wasting their morning.) Invitations should be sent to the News Desk and contacts on each paper several days in advance, giving time, date, address, information on what it is about and who will be speaking. If your organization is publishing a report, make sure that the journalists have copies in advance of the press conference, so that they can read it and ask relevant questions. If the charity's headquarters are not easily accessible to the press, then consideration should be given to the hiring of a reception room in a hotel or local hall. When the conference starts the chairman should welcome the press, introduce the other speakers and give a brief introduction on the purpose of the meeting. Then the main speaker should speak, for no more than ten minutes, introducing newsworthy information not included in the advance notice press release calling the conference. Plenty of time should be allowed for questions. Make sure that your speakers are direct and to the point. Refreshments may be served, but should be modest to be consistent with the charity's image.

If you are releasing information to the press in advance, make clear to them that the story is embargoed until a specific time on a specific day. The press are very good at keeping embargoes, but this works both ways—if you are placing an embargo on a story, do not give preferential treatment to one paper, allowing them to release the story before the embargo is lifted—this will alienate all the others.

A good way of securing publicity is to organize 'stunts', especially the sort which yield a good photograph. A few basic rules about publicity stunts should be noted: first, the more original the stunt the more likely you are to get press coverage; second, do not spend much money on stunts—a good stunt requires ingenuity, not funding. Remember that pretty girls, well-known people and children attract press photographers.

Do not be frightened of approaching the press. Newspapers need stories, and are generally sympathetic to charities; but to ensure that you do not dissipate this goodwill, at least with reference to your own charity, follow the basic rules outlined above in dealing with the press. If you want a record of press coverage of your charity, you could consider subscribing to a press cutting agency. This should not be necessary for a local charity, whose press coverage would be limited to a few newspapers. Press cutting agencies are listed as a category in the Yellow Pages; if there are none in your area, then contact the national agencies which are listed in the London (Central) Yellow Pages.

Advertising in the press and magazines

Over £1 million a year is spent by charities on press advertising alone. Press advertising is extremely costly: a full page advertisement in a national daily will cost several thousand pounds. Such expenditure should be undertaken with caution, especially as advertising is seen as a flagrant example of lavish spending by charities, and must be used with discretion. A charity should be able to show, if challenged, that its advertising was of value either in raising funds directly or by creating public awareness for its work.

The indispensable guide for advertisers is *BRAD (British Rate and Data)* which lists all newspapers, consumer periodicals and trade, technical and professional publications. It gives their advertising rates, and where available the circulation figures. It is useful in supplying information on journals of whose existence one is unaware, but which might serve relevant interest groups.

A charity must be clear as to why it is advertising. For most large charities, the reason is that they wish to ensure public awareness: to maintain their high incomes they must ensure that the charity's name and aims are kept before the public. Some charities (such as Oxfam and Shelter) have traditionally used advertising as a means of sustaining public awareness; others (such as the Red Cross) scarcely advertise at all. It is disturbing how little thought charities appear to give to their advertising. A study of ten major charities, each with annual incomes exceeding £1 million, showed that although these charities were responsible for placing more than half of all charity advertising, not all of them analysed the cost effectiveness of their advertising, and several admitted that the selection of newspapers in which to advertise was fairly random within the quality press.

As a general rule, advertising for funds is rarely successful. Charities are, not surprisingly, reluctant to reveal details of their unsuccessful advertising, because it lays them open to accusations of inefficiency and money wasting. In fact, relatively few charities make stringent analyses of the efficacy of their advertising campaigns, preferring to claim that the exercise won goodwill, if not cash. What analyses have been done show that major campaigns, such as that of Help The Aged, may be expected to recoup the cost of advertising by undertaking such large and sustained advertising programmes that the spin-off, in fund-raising terms, is considerable: it makes a charity's name and work so well known that its thrift shops, local fund-raising drives, etc., benefit, and legacy and covenant income can be expected to rise. This type of campaign presupposes large resources as there will be a time lag between the payment for advertising and the time money can be expected to be recouped.

It does not automatically follow that a large, sustained advertising campaign will recover its costs. There is little secret about the fact that Oxfam's recent campaigns have brought disappointing results, though earlier Oxfam campaigns were yielding a 20:1 return. This illustrates the problem of maintaining the urgency of one's appeal year after year, when the public is becoming dulled to the shocking photographs and startling headlines. A large-scale organization such as Oxfam, that has traditionally advertised extensively, finds itself in a cleft stick: it feels obliged to advertise to sustain its predominant position, but finds the effectiveness of its advertising decreases as it loses its shock value.

If large-scale advertising does not always bring success, the dabbling in advertising in which many charities indulge never succeeds. For example, a charity may decide it will advertise (perhaps for no better reason than that it sees other charities do so, and assumes that they must be successful). An advertisement, not particularly eye-catching, is drawn up and placed in the newspapers that the charity's administrators think of as most useful. Because of the high costs the advertisements appear only a few times. The whole exercise is a dismal failure, and yields very little response, either in terms of interest or funds, and ends in mutual recriminations by all involved.

For charities which are not spending five-figure budgets on advertising, it is a wise general principle to link advertising to a specific event (for example, if launching a report, or to back up a television or radio appeal). It is more effective to repeat small advertisements than to place one large advertisement for, if anything, it is the frequent repetition of a charity's name that fixes it in people's minds. In advertising, as in all forms of publicity, some basic precepts must be followed: project a positive image; show a distinct role; create sympathy for the charity's aims; and show that the charity can achieve its goals, given enough funds.

When deciding where to advertise, consider whom you wish to reach and what papers or magazines they read. (The circulation figures for each newspaper and magazine can be found in *BRAD*.) Take care not to assume that because newspaper A has a circulation four times greater than newspaper B, response from newspaper A readers will be four times greater: charities learn from experience that some newspapers have readership more sympathetic to their cause than others. Generally, the national press are the most costly—returns are often higher, in relation to cost, from the religious or provincial press.

If a charity is placing a substantial amount of advertising (say, over £3,000 per annum), it should consider using an advertising agency. The agency will advise on where to advertise, and should also provide design advice. Some agencies take on a few charity accounts at nominal cost, for prestige reasons. Most offer reduced rates for charities—but advertising agencies are not cheap.

Charities are not restricted to display advertising. Many use the personal columns, or, in the case of medical research charities, the Announcement of Deaths. It is often easier to recoup the cost of these 'classified' advertisements, but again this type of advertising campaign needs continuity. Get to know the differences between the styles of newspapers: an advertisement appropriate to the *Guardian* is unlikely to be suitable for the *Daily Mirror* or *News of the World*.

If undertaking the advertising without the advice of an agency, then try to devise an eye-catching advertisement, remembering the effectiveness of blank areas in a newspaper; keep the wording brief and always give people a positive choice—the feeling that they can help by donating. A sense of urgency also helps generate funds but is, of course, difficult to sustain over a long period. Photographs are often eye-catching, but involve the cost of making a block (at a cost of £10 upwards). For advice on design of the advertisement, it might be helpful to telephone the Creative Director of an advertising agency (listed in *BRAD*) and see if he would be willing to help. Some are bound to be hostile, but you only need one to say 'yes'. He may do it free or charge a small fee.

To sum up, advertising should be undertaken with caution, because of the high costs. Few charities find advertising suitable as a fund-raising method, but often justify it as creating 'awareness of the charity's work'. Small-scale, sporadic advertising is usually the least remunerative, except when linked to a particular event, such as the launching of a report. Design of the advertisements is crucial, and advice should be sought. Care must be taken in selection of a suitable medium. Advertisements should be in keeping with the image of the charity, and stimulate a positive response.

Television programmes

Television has a very large audience and so the value of television coverage as a means of publicity can be readily appreciated. One has only to think of the role of *Cathy Come Home* in popularizing the plight of the homeless and thus establishing Shelter, to realize the tremendous impact that television publicity can have.

To secure television coverage of a charity's work and promotions, one follows much the same procedure as in dealing with the press. Press releases should be sent to the television companies (listed in the *PR Planner*) as well as to newspapers. Remember, if it is an event of local interest, send it to the regional office of the television company; if of national interest, send it to the national company. If the item is a news item, then send it (or telephone it) to 'News Intake'. If it is of interest to a specific programme, then send it to the producer of that particular programme. Just as you must learn about the various newspapers before you can place stories efficiently, so you must learn about the varying needs of different television programmes. (It might, on occasion, be useful to know which programmes have the highest ratings—this information can be found in *Campaign*, the paper of the advertising industry.) If you are seeking advance publicity, then send details to the 'Future Events Unit'. Give plenty of notice, especially if you are hoping for outside coverage. Television, as a medium, clearly lends itself to coverage of 'stunts', which provide interesting pictures. Whether the television companies pick up your press releases or not will depend on how new or interesting they are, or, to some extent, just on luck—whether it is a busy or slack time, and if the subject takes the producer's fancy. At best your overall publicity will accumulate such interest in your activities that they will make a documentary about them; at worst, they will do an *exposé*!

Two television programmes provide a special service to charities—'Blue Peter' (BBC) and 'Magpie' (Thames TV). These are both children's programmes, and both launch an annual appeal for a project on behalf of a charity, in late November/early December. Both programmes maintain the rule that an individual charity is not named. For example, they have appealed for deaf children and spina bifida children, without naming the agencies through whom they found the projects and which will disburse the funds. The method of selecting projects seems similar: it is determined by those working on the programme, after taking into account viewers' letters and applications by charities for specific projects. Neither considers appeals for running costs, but prefers capital projects. 'Magpie' appeals for funds, whereas 'Blue Peter' asks viewers to send in items, such as scrap metal or old books or stamps, which can be sold.

'Magpie's' first appeal was in 1970, and yielded £9,000 for mentally handicapped children. In 1971, £30,000 was raised for deaf children; in 1972, £80,000 for spina bifida children; and in 1973, £70,700 was raised for autistic children. 'Magpie' likes to confine appeals to causes in the United Kingdom, and prefers children's charities (though it says it is prepared to consider overseas aid and sections of the community other than children). Any charity with a suitable capital project should write to the programme by August, for appeals to be launched in late November or early December.

'Blue Peter's' first appeal was in 1962, yielding 100 sacks of toys to be given to poor children, but the appeals have expanded enormously since then. One consistent feature has been that the target has been doubled, trebled or quadrupled. Thus the 1966 appeal for paperback books for re-cycling, which sought to buy one inland rescue craft, in fact brought enough to buy four such boats. The range of causes supported is much greater than that of 'Magpie': it has varied from holiday cabins for handicapped children, hot dinner vans for old people, to medical supplies to developing countries. There are no geographical limitations, nor are they limited to children. If you have a suitable capital project, then send an application to the producer of 'Blue Peter'.

Apart from the funds gained by having your charity selected for a 'Blue Peter' or 'Magpie' appeal, one must also understand the tremendous value of the publicity gained. The appeal is launched with a great deal of background information and television coverage, and the educational value is enormous. Both programmes have large audiences.

Television appeals

Both BBC and ITV give television time to appeals by individual charities. BBV TV allows fourteen such appeals a year, and ITV twelve. The rules governing such appeals are common to both organizations, and indeed they share the same Appeals Advisory Committee. The reasons for broadcasting appeals are stated by the BBC as 'providing a service to those members of the public who are charitably inclined, on the proven assumption that such people would welcome authoritative information and guidance as to causes deserving of their support and secondly quite simply to raise money for good causes and encourage the habit of giving'.

The Appeals Advisory Committee uses the following criteria in granting appeals:

1. As a general rule the charity should be concerned directly, or indirectly through preventive work, with alleviating human suffering or alternatively aim to promote social, physical, cultural, mental or moral well-being. (For the sake of variety, animal charities or charities to preserve the national heritage may be included.)
2. A charity should have gained or be likely to gain public support.
3. It should be registered with the Charity Commissioners.
4. It should have achieved, or have a good prospect of achieving a stable position in the charitable world.
5. It must demonstrate a need for funds for specified purposes which cannot be provided from income or reserve.
6. The charitable work of religious organizations may be eligible, if the charitable and not the religious work is the primary object of the appeal.
7. Restoration or repairs of cathedrals and churches of genuine historical and architectural interest is eligible, but not new buildings or extension work.
8. Memorial funds are not recommended unless set up for charitable purposes of great general interest.
9. Hospitals outside the National Health Service can be considered, as can 'Friends' of hospitals, provided they are appealing for projects not covered by the NHS.
10. Educational charities are not considered unless their work has some special social content.
11. An appeal will not be allowed where the benefits are confined to members of a trade or profession, except

where there is some special connection with broadcasting or the beneficiaries may be thought to have some special claim to public support, e.g. nurses, police.

12. Organizations existing primarily to raise funds for other bodies to spend are considered with special care.
13. Charities benefiting particular regions are not normally eligible for a national appeal.

If your charity fulfils the above criteria, then application may be made to, for the BBC, the Appeals Secretary, The BBC, Broadcasting House, London W1, or, for ITV, the Appeals Secretary, The Independent Broadcasting Authority, 70 Brompton Road, London SW3. (Scotland has its own Appeals Advisory Committee, so apply to the Scottish Broadcasting Authorities.) Applications should be accompanied by audited accounts and the latest annual report of the charity. The Appeals Advisory Committee considers all applications for appeals three times a year, and the appeals programme is worked out about six months in advance. Both BBC and ITV have the rule that a charity may not re-apply for an appeal, even if it was unsuccessful in securing one, within two years. There is nothing to stop a charity applying for an appeal to the BBC in year 1, then again in year 3, and applying to the IBA in years 2 and 4. In exceptional circumstances in fact, both BBC and ITV waive this rule: the exceptions may be made on the grounds that (a) the organization is mainly dependent on

Table 2 *Some examples of ITV appeals*

Date	Cause	Person making appeal	Amount raised	No. of donations
1974:	Lepra	Gerald Harper	£18,000*	(unrecorded)
Feb.	Elderly Invalids Fund	Jimmy Saville	£22,690	2,284
Mar.	RNLI	Michael Bentine	£1,980	719
Apr.	Winston Churchill Memorial Trust	Lady Soames	£631	—
May	London Assoc. for the Blind	Hughie Green	£8,004	3,886

Table 2 *cont.*

Date	Cause	Person making appeal	Amount raised	No. of donations
Jun.	British Polio Fellowship	William Franklyn	£5,101	5,034
Jul.	Helping Hand Organization	Peter Adamson	£653	–
Sep.	Queen Elizabeth's Foundation for the Disabled	Kenneth More	£4,330	1,784
Oct.	L'Arche	Sylvia Syms	£4,212	1,807
Nov.	CURE	Sheila Hancock	£538	293
Dec.	Mental Health Trust & Research Fund	Gordon Jackson	£2,520	–
Dec.‡	Royal Society for the Prevention of Accidents	Jimmy Young	£625	–
1975:				
Jan.	Sunfield Children's Homes	Brian Rix	£15,047	2,144
Feb.	Leukaemia Research Fund	John Mills	£11,077	1,147
Mar.	Providence (Row) Night Refuge & Home	Eamonn Andrews	£4,755	1,951
Apr.	Shelter	Ronnie Barker	£2,007	598
Jun.	Elizabeth Fitzroy Homes for the Handicapped Trust	Hughie Green	£3,059	922
Jun.	Belfast Cathedral Chapel of Unity	Sam Kydd	£282	–
Jul.	Kidney Research Unit for Wales Foundation	Keith Macklin	£1,041	251
Aug.	Possum Users' Association	Les Dawson†	£3,120	1,000

* Two years before Lepra raised only £6,000. They had backed the 1974 appeal with advertising, but both Lepra and the IBA were surprised by the response.

‡ Combined results of ITV and BBC Radio.

† Compare BBC TV appeal, Jan. 1974, for the same cause—raised £28,281.

the proceeds of broadcast appeals, (b) if a number of organizations combine to present a joint appeal, then individual appeals need not always be precluded thereafter, (c) if a special need arises that could not have been foreseen at the time of earlier appeals. Special additional appeals may be allowed if there is a disaster at home or abroad, on condition that either a national fund is set up or the UK Disasters Emergency Committee approves the appeal. (This consists of Oxfam, the Red Cross, War on Want, Save the Children Fund and Christian Aid.)

Once an appeal has been granted, the charity can depend upon a great deal of help in preparing the appeal from the television companies themselves. ITV does not produce the appeal itself; instead, four of its constituent companies (London Weekend, ATV, Granada and Yorkshire Televisions) take it in turn to produce four special appeal broadcasts at a time.

There seem to be two factors crucial to determining the success of a television appeal: first, the cause itself (those in which the beneficiaries are thought to have 'brought it on themselves', such as alcoholics or drug addicts, do least well), and, second, the personality of the person making the appeal. Appeals in the summer generally do worse than those at other times. Generally, ITV appeals are expected to yield less than those on BBC.

The BBC make available records of appeals since 1971. The results of 1973/4 appeals are reproduced here to show not only the different amounts raised but also the type of person asked to make the appeals and the variety of causes.

Some appeals do predictably badly, like the National Gypsy Education Council and the National Council for One Parent Families; others, like the Malcolm Sargent Cancer Fund for Children, do predictably well. But the results of the Simon Community Trust appeal in November 1972 which raised over £17,000 show that an apparently unpopular cause can be made attractive, with a little ingenuity: the appeal showed children with animals on the Simon Community Farm, an aspect of its work not usually known. Care should be taken in selecting the right person to make the appeal. Television news readers and actors appear prime favourites. What is needed, it seems, is an authoritative manner, to instil confidence in the viewer.

Table 3 *BBC TV appeals*

Date	Cause	Person making appeal	Amount raised
1973:			
Jan.	Friedreich's Ataxia Group	Patrick Allen	£28,827
Feb.	Refresh	Patrick Moore	£38,858
Mar.	Ely Cathedral	Richard Baker	£4,914
Apr.	Task Force	Clive Dunn	£1,086
May	Variety Club of Great Britain	Ronnie Corbett	£3,099
Jun.	Coventry Corrymeela Venture	David Kossoff	£3,594
Jul.	Royal National Lifeboat Institution	Raymond Baxter	£8,245
Aug.	Universities Federation of Animal Welfare	John Hillaby	£6,228
Sep.	Malcolm Sargent Cancer Fund for Children	Jack Hedley	£27,657
Oct.	St Christopher's Hospice (South East only)	Sheila Hancock	£11,542
Oct.	Emergency Appeal, Ethiopian and African Drought (also on ITV)	Jonathan Dimbleby	£1,400,000
Nov.	Muscular Dystrophy Group of Great Britain	Richard Attenborough	£31,012
Nov.	Children in Need of Help (BBC's own appeal)	Geoffrey Wheeler	£4,405
Dec.	MIND (National Assoc. for Mental Health)	Billie Whitelaw	£10,014
Xmas Day	National Council for One Parent Families	Harry Secombe	£903*

Table 3 *cont.*

Date	Cause	Person making appeal	Amount raised
1974:			
Jan.	Possum Users' Association	Cliff Morgan	£28,281
Feb.	Women's National Cancer Control Campaign	Judith Chalmers	£12,000
Mar.	Forces Help Soc. & Lord Roberts Workshops	Dame Anna Neagle	£8,500
Apr.	Women's Holiday Fund (S.E. only)	Jack Warner	£3,300
May	Winston Churchill Memorial Trust (TV & Radio 4)	Winston Churchill, MP	£3,090
May	The Samaritans	Glenda Jackson	£4,589
Jun.	Queen's Nursing Institute	Roy Hudd	£1,389
Jul.	Bath Preservation Trust	Lord Clark	£2,958
Aug.	Disabled Drivers' Association	Graham Hill	£3,909
Sep.	Camphill Village Trust	Richard Whitmore	£23,560
Sep.	Emergency Appeal: Honduras Hurricane (TV/R4/IBA & Nat. Press)	James Cameron	£338,000
Oct.	National Society for Epileptics (S.E. only)	Tony Brandon	£3,673
Nov.	Age Concern	Jack Warner	£13,361
Nov.	Children in Need of Help (TV & Radio 4)	Esther Rantzen	£20,752
Dec.	Inskip St Giles Housing Association	Frank Bough	£8,122
Xmas Day	National Deaf Children's Soc.	Dame Flora Robson	£2,892

* Despite extensive back-up newspaper advertising.

L

Apart from the financial gain of an appeal, one must also consider the publicity value. Even if people do not give on this occasion, it may predispose them to give in the future. For some charities a television appeal provides a good opportunity to make people aware of their existence: the charity is, paradoxically, using the appeal to reach its beneficiaries rather than its donors.

Television advertising

In the unlikely event that your charity should wish to advertise on commercial television, then the addresses of each company and the rates are listed in *BRAD*. Television advertising cannot, without contravening the charter, attempt to raise funds, but can increase awareness of a charity's work.

Radio

The rules for securing radio coverage are much the same as for television. Local radio stations, both commercial and non-commercial, are, like local newspapers, usually pleased to publicize your charity's activities. The names and addresses of local and national radio stations can be found in the *PR Planner*. The music/chat shows on Radios One and Two may provide an opportunity for more trivial items. Magazine programmes, such as 'Woman's Hour', may pick up items of more weight, and the news programmes should be sent all press releases you are sending to the national press. Just as you should get to know the different requirements of the different newspapers, and the different television programmes, so you should learn about the needs of various radio programmes. Send, or telephone, items to the producer of the programme on which you hope to secure coverage. If the information may be of interest to several programmes, then send it to all of them. In the unlikely event of your charity wishing to advertise on commercial radio, you can find the rates listed in *BRAD*.

The BBC broadcasts, on Radio Four, an appeal 53 times a year. Charities are selected by the same method as for television appeals. The list of appeals for the first quarter of 1973 and second quarter of 1975 show the variety of causes, the amounts raised and those who made the appeals—see Table 4. Like the television appeals, the amounts vary, influenced by the popularity of the cause and

Table 4 *BBC Radio appeals*

Date	Cause	Person making appeal	Amount raised
1973:			
7 Jan.	Searchlight Workshops	Alan Melville	£1,573
14 Jan.	Family Service Units	Bishop of Stepney	£1,708
21 Jan.	(ex. Scotland) Abbeyfield Soc.	Dame Anna Neagle	£3,900
28 Jan.	Soldiers', Sailors' and Airmen's Families Assoc.	Peter West	£1,239
4 Feb.	St Luke's Nursing Home for Clergy	Derek Nimmo	£2,140
11 Feb.	Cystic Fibrosis Research Trust	Leslie Crowther	£2,793
18 Feb.	(ex. Scotland) Peterborough Cathedral	John Betjeman	£635
25 Feb.	British Sailors' Society	Geoffrey Wheeler	£1,302
4 Mar.	Industrial Therapy Organization	J. M. Hargreaves	£817
11 Mar.	Society of St Dismas	Lord Longford	£1,255
18 Mar.	(ex. Scotland) Invalid Children's Aid Association	Nanette Newman	£1,381
25 Mar.	Parkinson's Disease Society	Bill Simpson	£4,711
1975:			
6 Apr.	(Radio 4: England) St Giles' Centre	Andrew Cruickshank	£1,816.37
	(Radio 4: Scotland) The Salvation Army	Brig. Thomas Cheadle	£1,717.54
	(Radio 4: Wales) Swansea Youth Enterprise	Dennis Mills	£215
	(Radio 4: N. Ireland)		

Table 4 *cont.*

Date	Cause	Person making appeal	Amount raised
6 Apr.	Northern Ireland Council on Riding for the Disabled	Ernest McMillen	£122.60
13 Apr.	(Radio 4, ex. Scotland) Children's Country Holiday Fund	Mrs Pauline Crabbe	£1,797.81
	(Radio 4: Scotland) James Little College Ltd for Physically Handicapped	Revd. James Currie	£552.81
20 Apr.	(Radio 4, ex Scotland) Leukaemia Research Fund	Hattie Jacques	£3,495.58
	(Radio Midlands) The Friends of Summerfield Hospital	Beryl Reid	£1,467
	(Radio E. Anglia) Leeway Norwich Women's Refuge	Susanne Hall	£900
	(Radio North) Cripples' Help Society (Manchester & Leeds)	Mike Yarwood	£1,132.35
	(Radio North – Newcastle) Tyneside Challenge Club for Physically Disabled Children	Brendan Foster	£738
	(Radio West) Kennet & Avon Canal Trust	John Snagge	£148.55
	(Radio South) Le Court Cheshire Home	Richard Baker	£1,720
	(Radio S. West) Gulworthy School for Autistic Children	Joe Pengelly	£802.12

Table 4 *cont.*

Date	Cause	Person making appeal	Amount raised
27 Apr.	(Radio 4: ex. Scotland) Family Welfare Association	Mrs Patricia Thomas	£597.18
	(Radio 4: Scotland) Leukaemia Research Fund (Scotland)	Russell Hunter	£1,008.27
4 May	(Radio 4: England) Portfield School for Autistic Children	Mrs Betty Peters	£1,735
	(Radio 4: Scotland) Glasgow City Mission	William McDowall	£603.04
	(Radio 4: Wales) Boys' Clubs of Wales	John Selby	£421.86
	(Radio 4: N. Ireland) British Red Cross Society	Cicely Mathews	£60
11 May	(Radio 4: ex. Scotland) Cecil Houses (Inc.)	Roy Hay	£1,091.92
	(Radio 4: Scotland) Barony Housing Assoc.	Jean Harland	£70
18 May	(Radio 4: ex. Scotland) Selby Abbey	The Bishop of Selby	£1,350
25 May	(Radio 4) British Library of Tape Recordings for Hospital Patients	Frank Muir	£1,243.37
1 Jun.	(Radio 4: England & N. Ireland) Salisbury Diocesan Association for the Deaf and Hard of Hearing	The Bishop of Sherborne	£4,446.56

Table 4 *cont.*

Date	Cause	Person making appeal	Amount raised
1 Jun.	(Radio 4: Scotland) The National Trust for Scotland	The Earl of Wemyss & March	£80.65
	(Radio 4: Wales) Swansea Little Theatre	Peter Davies	£91.61
8 Jun.	(Radio 4) Parkinson's Disease Society	Bill Simpson	£3,792*
15 Jun.	(Radio 4: ex. Scotland) Church of England Council for Social Aid	Archie Hill	£1,553.72
	(Radio 4: Scotland) Action Research for the Crippled Child	Dame Anna Neagle	£380.60
22 Jun.	(Radio 4) Far East Fund	Kenneth More	£3,840
Jun.	(Radio 4: ex. Scotland) St Christopher's School, Bristol	Johnny Morris	£3,035.09
	(Radio 4: Scotland) Edinburgh City Mission	Albert Long	£519.50

* Compare Radio 4 appeal, March 1973, for same cause—raised £4,711.

the person making the appeal, and depending on the success of the broadcast in overcoming prejudice against the cause—and on a large measure of luck. Two annual appeals (on Christmas Day for the Wireless for the Blind Fund and in the week before Christmas for the St Martin's-in-the-Fields Christmas Fund) regularly top £20,000 each, so the value of radio appeals must not be underestimated.

Posters

Charities can and do use posters to publicize their cause in an enormous variety of situations—on street hoardings, train stations, the London underground, buses throughout the country. Poster advertising has two main virtues—it is relatively cheap, and it is reckoned that the individual poster is seen a good many times by the same person, so the message is hammered home. Posters do not, in themselves, put over the appeal, but they remind people of its existence.

The British Poster Association have since the beginning of the century operated their charity scheme, through which their member companies (throughout the UK) give £14 million worth of free poster sites a year. The BPA will, on application, consider requests for free sites to be given to a charity's campaign for one month. (If the sites are not booked by someone else at the end of the month, then the charity's poster just remains on view till covered by the next client's poster.) This is not granted automatically. The BPA scheme presupposes that the charity will undertake a fairly large-scale campaign (at least 5,000–6,000 double crown posters or 2,000–3,000 4-sheet posters), not just the odd posters. (The charity may have a combination of any two—double crown or 4-sheet or 16-sheet—posters, but not all three sizes.) If the charity wants a smaller number of sites, especially if limited to one locality, then the BPA will pass the request on to its member companies in that area, if they think the charity's application suitable.

If a charity is spending considerable amounts of money on other types of advertising, then the BPA is not likely to be wholly sympathetic to the suggestion that poster sites should be included free of charge. In such circumstances they are likely to suggest an arrangement such as giving one free site for every one paid for. There is a waiting list for charities which wish to take advantage of the BPA scheme. Normally charities should apply about six months in advance.

The BPA retain the right to refuse to display certain posters, should they consider them indecent. They appear to maintain a rather traditional view of indecency. The official view is that the BPA will not accept anything too horrific. Other controllers of poster sites are similarly squeamish. London Transport's dislike of nipples is notorious. But few charities are likely to encounter this hostility, since a common criticism of charities' advertising is that it is too pedestrian.

Apart from roadside hoardings, which can be obtained through the BPA, posters can be displayed at British Rail stations, on trains, on hovercraft, at British Transport Hotels, and on buses, through British Transport Advertising, 17 Newman Street, London W1. The BTA does not operate a charity scheme like the BPA, but will give a 25 per cent reduction on site hiring charges for charities.

For poster advertising on London Transport, including tube trains, at tube stations and on buses, London Transport Advertising should be contacted. They give no charity discount, but will (subject to the availability of space) give up to 25 per cent 'overshow'—i.e. space in addition to that paid for, *if the charity asks for it.*

Obtaining suitable sites for posters is only half the problem. There remains the need to secure a good design. It is unlikely that a charity will be able to design its own posters, unless they have a tame artist, and for most it will be necessary to enlist the help of an advertising agency. Through discussions with the agency, the charity should make clear what it wants the poster to achieve—in terms of the image it wants to project. Clearly posters, since seen briefly, must be simple, uncluttered, and immediate in their impact. Imagination is the quality most needed. A series of posters which have been outstanding are those issued by the Health Education Council. They have included the pregnant boy (as an advertisement for more considerate family planning), and a nude pregnant woman seen smoking (highlighting the bad effects of smoking on the foetus). Both posters are so visually incongruous that they are immediately arresting. They have been unacceptable to those controlling the poster sites, yet have secured (because they aroused such controversy) extensive exposure in the press. It is an ironic position—that they failed to secure coverage in the medium they intended, but reached the public more effectively through the other media.

Although poster sites can, through the goodwill of the BPA, be secured free, the cost of producing the posters must still be found. It is difficult to secure estimates for the printing costs of posters, since the cost depends on quantities (as with all printing, it becomes progressively cheaper the larger the number to be printed), and the number of colours used. As a very rough general guide:

2,500 × 4-sheet posters in 2-colour line would cost about	£600
in 4-colour half-tone (i.e. reproducing photographs)	£1,500
2,500 × 16-sheet posters in 2-colour line would cost about	£2,500
in 4-colour half-tone	£3,500

Also to be considered as posters are car stickers. These can be cheaply produced, will generally carry a very simple message—either just the name of the charity or perhaps a slogan like 'I'm a Shelter Helper' or 'Join the War on Want'. Most charities will be able to devise suitable car stickers, without needing professional advice as to design. Car stickers can be very effective in keeping a charity's name in the public mind. They also produce an atmosphere of success, when large numbers of cars are seen to bear a charity's stickers—it helps the band waggoning effect. To be effective, car stickers must be widely used: one or two will make no impact—unless the stickers are widely seen people will assume they are advertising the name of a garage.

People can be asked to put car stickers, or any other posters, in their windows, as is done at election time. This form of publicity is especially valuable for local charities which seek to increase local involvement. Remember, a lone, forlorn poster is unlikely to have impact: attempts must be made to have a significant number of posters up, if the whole enterprise is not to project an image of dismal failure.

Promotional films

Increasingly, large charities have been commissioning films (about twenty minutes long) to promote their cause. The promotional film is designed to be used by a speaker representing the charity, to highlight his appeal. Film, especially in our society which is so accustomed to receiving information through television, is an easy method to get across what one's charity is about, and through the style of the film will say much of the charity's style of work. It is generally easier to retain an audience's interest through film rather than by a talk, unless the speaker is exceptionally good. The promotional film prepares the ground for the speaker to make an appeal for funds.

The success, in terms of impact, of any film must depend on its being shown. Before commissioning a film, make sure that your charity can secure 'speaking engagements' at which a film could be shown. Most charities have some requests for speakers, from Rotary Clubs, women's groups and schools, and the level of the existing demand is some guide as to whether it would be useful to commission a promotional film—although a charity can increase the demand for speakers with an increase in general publicity, for people will want to learn more of a charity's work once their appetites for information have been whetted. It is also open to charities to write to various organizations, offering to send a speaker: the offer to show a film can increase the attractiveness of the proposal. If your charity could not undertake to supply speakers (through lack of personnel), it is not really sensible to commission a promotional film, since it cannot be shown. Of course, a newly made film would be a suitable topic for a press show, and might create interest in that way, leading to requests to see the film.

Once you have determined to commission a film, approach the Film Production Association of Great Britain, 27 Soho Street, London W1, who will be able to recommend suitable film companies to you. The Association will also advise on the making of cartoons and of short films, suitable for cinema advertising. It is difficult to forecast how much a film will cost, as this depends on whether it is shot on location, in Africa or Accrington, whether it is in colour or black-and-white, and the level of sophisticated filming which may require a large crew. As a general guide, perhaps it is helpful to say that a twenty-minute film is unlikely to cost less than £5,000. Cartoons are generally more expensive. In addition, the charity may have to incur the expense of hiring a projector to show the film, at least on some occasions.

If the charity wants to make an advertising film, to be shown at cinemas, it should first ascertain the current rate for showing such a film—the names of the relevant companies can be found in *BRAD*, under the listing 'cinema advertising'.

Most charities have found promotional films very worthwhile, and have been able to recoup the cost of making the film. But some have been disappointed in the film itself, feeling that the film producer has not made the best possible case for the charity. Remember his ability to do so will depend on how well he is briefed. Be clear in your own mind what aspects of your work you would like emphasized and how you want your charity's image projected. (There will clearly need to be different approaches if the film is to be shown to school children or lawyers or doctors.) It is almost certain that you will want to project a warm, caring image, but you should also give some thought to whether you want to seem young, radical and somewhat irreverent, or perhaps mature and stately. These questions of a charity's style must be understood by the charity itself, so that the film producer can project this image. That is, of course, essential in briefing any outside help.

Leaflets

Every charity, if it hopes to solicit funds, needs a simple leaflet to provide information on the charity's aims. Leaflets are needed to be sent out with appeal letters, can be handed out at public meetings, delivered door-to-door, or included as inserts with other publications. Under the heading 'leaflets' will be included everything from the one-page, duplicated sheet to the twenty-page glossy brochure.

When considering the need for a leaflet, the first thing to decide is what it should say. Two common faults should be avoided. The first is to fix the size of the leaflet without having regard to how much real information the leaflet will contain, so that the compiler has four pages to fill with two-and-a-half pages of information. The result is a scrappy, sparse leaflet. Work out what information should be included before deciding on size. The second common mistake is to try to make the leaflet suitable for an audience ranging from twelve-year-old school children to seventy-year-old lawyers—the end result is usually so bland as to be meaningless to most readers. It is better to try to identify the readership of a leaflet with some accuracy, and to angle the contents accordingly.

Any leaflet, as all the promotional material on the charity, should reflect its image and style. It should not be over-glossy or slick: the charity is not trying to compete with industry in professionalism, but should strive for a professionalism that is appropriate. There is no doubt that too glossy a leaflet is counter-productive—it makes potential donors feel that their money would be misspent, or is not really needed.

Photographs are usually more eloquent than prose, but should not be used indiscriminately, as they can add to the printing costs. It should not be assumed that as photographs are effective, all photographs will be effective. Do not use a photograph simply because it is easily accessible. Make the effort to find a really first class photograph which tells a great deal about your cause and where possible shows your charity's achievements. If you do not have any suitable pictures, then consider commissioning a photographer or using photograph libraries—notably the Radio Times Hulton Picture Library, to find something in their records. Always be on the lookout for good photographs in newspapers and magazines, which are usually sympathetic to requests to allow the pictures to be reproduced by a charity. Avoid the mistake of using photographs as space-fillers for odd corners: the reader's eye is drawn first to pictures, so they must be interesting enough to make him want to read the main body of the leaflet. A device used very frequently by charities is to use children in photographs, on the assumption that they provoke an emotional, sentimental response.

Include in a leaflet information designed to interest someone new to the field. Generally speaking, people want to know:

1. What the problem is—how many people it affects;
2. What the causes of the problem are—if they are unknown, what is being done to discover them and, if known, what is being done to overcome them;
3. What the charity is doing to solve the problem—and what it hopes to do if more funds are forthcoming;
4. There should also be included some information on how the reader could help other than by sending a donation, for example, by forming an aid group, sending in trading stamps, signing a covenant, becoming a voluntary worker for the charity.

In many cases it is appropriate to include in a leaflet a tear-off slip for a donation or covenant form and information on legacies. The address of the charity should always be prominently displayed so that potential donors are not deterred by not knowing where to send their contributions.

The cost of leaflets will obviously depend on the size and design. Some points to note, in keeping down the cost, are to choose the lightest quality paper appropriate for the job. The lighter the paper the cheaper it is, and consequently card is expensive. Shiny paper is usually more expensive than matt, but as a general rule it is sensible to ask the printer in case he has any paper he wishes to use up, which he will offer at reduced rate. Similarly, ask the printer which size paper fits his machines, since if you specify a size inconvenient to him there will be wastage of paper and therefore of funds. Similarly, use a size of leaflet that will fit into a standard envelope, to avoid the cost of having special envelopes. Do not devise elaborately folded leaflets—this adds to the cost. For tear-off forms, consider whether a dotted line would suffice, or would perforation be essential—it adds to the cost. One colour printing is much cheaper than two or more colours, and remember that the one colour can be other than black. Photographs (which the printer refers to as half-tones) add to the cost, so use them with care—the number of photographs, not just the number of pages with photographs on, adds to the costs. It is sensible to ask your printer when his quiet season is, as he will often offer a discount for work which keeps machines busy during slack times.

Take care not to over-order the number of leaflets. Remember you will have to send out different material each time you mail to donors. It is better to order smaller amounts of a leaflet, and to up-date it frequently, rather than have numbers kept in stock. In the contract with the printer will be a clause allowing him to over-print on your order up to 10 per cent. In fact, he will probably over-print about 5 per cent, so bear this in mind when calculating the numbers of leaflets to order.

For design advice, it is usual to rely on the design team of your advertising agency. Make it clear to them what you want before you start, as any wasted effort on their part is likely to appear on your bill. If you do not use an advertising agency, and do not have enough work to warrant using one, try to secure a professional designer. Telephone the Creative Director of an advertising agency (listed in *BRAD*) and ask for his advice. He may be flattered enough to give it free. Other possibilities for securing a designer are a request to a teacher of graphics at the local art school, or a letter to the local paper asking for someone willing and able to help to contact you. It is possible to design a leaflet without a professional designer, but unless someone at the charity has a particular flair for design (and there is often a discrepancy between their real skill and their estimation of it), it is often difficult to achieve a suitable layout. If you cannot find a designer, and feel uncertain as to layout, then perhaps the best general rule is plagiarism. Look at the leaflets of other charities and see if any of them strike you as effective, and try to think why, and emulate them accordingly.

As a final note on leaflets, it is perhaps wise to remember that when sending receipts, a leaflet can be included in the same envelope for a minimal extra cost. It is often sensible to design a leaflet for this purpose—either a progress report or, alternatively, a leaflet on how to help the charity in ways other than donating. For example, you can appeal for used postage stamps, or urge people to form groups, or join a rally to publicize the charity's activities. Remember to keep people interested, and encouraged, by the charity's achievements, made possible through the donor's gift.

Apart from mailings, leaflets can be distributed in a variety of ways. Information on distributing leaflets through inserts in magazines can be found in *BRAD*. Not all magazines will have inserts. Some commercial firms will undertake leaflet drops on a house-to-house basis. Generally a charity should be able to recruit volunteers to do this, but if not, look up the firms in the Yellow Pages under 'publicity specialists', amongst whom they will be found.

Summary

A charity's publicity must predispose people to give to its cause; its fund-raising is designed to give them frequent opportunity to do so. An unknown cause cannot hope for funds. Publicity should not simply seek to maximize short-term giving: it should also have a long-term educational effect. Always project a positive image. Show that money can help the problem, and that your particular charity will spend any donations effectively. Emphasize the importance of the work, and by implication show why your charity should be supported rather than any other.

The forms of publicity are enormous, and include national, local and specialist press, both through editorial coverage and paid advertising, television and radio, local and national, through news coverage and special appeals. The charity can distribute its own publicity material, such as posters, promotional films and leaflets. Careful thought should be given to all aspects of publicity—they are the charity's public face, and can harm its cause.

12 Fund-raising consultants

If a charity's trustees are convinced of the need for more funds, and of their inability to raise them by themselves or using existing staff, then they can choose between calling in a firm of fund-raising consultants or appointing a fund-raiser to the staff of the charity. Before a decision is reached, the trustees (or whoever is responsible for the decision) should give fullest consideration to what image of the charity they want projected; from whom support is most likely to come; and, specifically, what the financial needs of the charity are likely to be over the quinquennium. Unless these questions are resolved, whoever is given the job of fund-raising will be working to an incomplete brief, and the results are unlikely to be felicitous.

The shortage of funds which will have generated the sense of crisis and forced the trustees and staff to call in consultants, or appoint a fund-raiser, can help an appeal, as, for once, those connected with the charity will expect to be asked to help with fund-raising. One thing any fund-raiser tackling a charity new to him will do is examine carefully the fund-raising potential of those associated with the charity, and see that it is fully exploited. The decision to appoint either a fund-raiser or consultants will have broken the inertia which may have hung over the charity's fund-raising for years. But do not expect the appointment of a fund-raiser or consultants to be the solution to all the charity's problems. If the charity is badly administered, if its work will not stand public scrutiny, then the fund-raiser cannot be expected to succeed. And do not expect funds to flow in the day after the fund-raiser or consultants walk through the door—it is fair to expect a six-month preparatory period.

The alternatives

1. A fund-raiser appointed to the staff

It is hard to find good fund-raisers. A small pool of experienced people switch charities, but many more feel that they can fund-raise and learn that they cannot at the expense of the charity. A lot of people have some experience of fund-raising, ranging from organizing a village fête to running a university rag. But their experience may be irrelevant to the type of fund-raising your charity needs, or the event may have succeeded despite their efforts. The problem of finding good fund-raisers is aggravated by the inability of many charity trustees to assess the competence of those applying for the job. Distrust glib plans to make thousands of pounds from pop concerts or confident generalizations on how the money will flow in as a result of an advertisement in *The Times*—value common sense above all other qualities.

It is crucial to appoint the right person for the job, as they stand as a public representative of the charity. If the charity's image is rather staid and conservative, and the main support is expected from middle-class, middle-aged people, then choose someone who will be at ease with such people. Similarly, if the main appeal is to young people, be sure to find someone who will mobilize them, and not deter them.

Be clear exactly what you want your fund-raiser to do. For example, if the charity has a very strong, dedicated group of trustees, who are willing to ask their peer group for funds but are too busy to undertake the administrative side of the job (receipting, servicing covenants, sending out annual reports), then what is needed is an administrator rather than a fund-raiser. The person appointed might be expected to organize balls or film premieres, but would not be expected to sell the tickets. Their job would be akin to that of a secretary to a committee.

One word about 'contacts': there are two schools of thought about the value of contacts. The one believes it is what fund-raising is all about; the other feels that it is rare for contacts to be of actual use. Generally, one can discount the value of the contacts of paid fund-raisers. They should have the knowledge of where to go, whom to ask and how to set about a campaign. They should not have to rely on their contacts, as the field of operation should be continually widening. It is for the trustees of the charity to exploit their contacts, not to expect their fund-raisers to have them. It is rare for 'contacts' to switch support from one charity to the other, to follow the fund-raiser's change of job. The sort of person who can boast the Queen Mother, Richard Burton and the head of ICI as his patrons is unlikely to be working as a paid fund-raiser.

When appointing a fund-raiser, make a real assessment of the cost involved—budgeting for postage, printing, secretarial help, cost of office space, etc. It is unrealistic to think the cost is simply the salary + National Insurance stamps. It may be that the cost involved will spur the trustees to a final effort to raise the money themselves.

One final word on appointing fund-raisers: be prepared to fire them if they are no good: a charity cannot afford the luxury of a useless member of staff. But before firing them, make sure that it is their fault and not the organization's that things have not gone well. Remember that the need to fire someone means that the trustees have made a bad choice in the first place, and that the person dismissed is having to suffer as a result of it.

2. *Fund-raising consultants*

Consultants can be employed for a 'one-off' campaign, as consultants to give general advice or retained as permanent advisers, though the last is unusual. A firm will usually appoint a Campaign Director from amongst its staff to direct the charity's appeal, and should be able to provide back-up staff to give expert advice on relevant aspects of the work, such as appeals to trusts, the preparation of publicity material, or covenant campaigns. The calibre of the personnel, and the advice they can give, varies enormously from one firm of consultants to the other. There is no professional body to enforce even minimal standards of competence, and the high turnover in staff in fund-raising consultancies may mean that the staff is not sufficiently expert to offer the service the firm would claim. Appointing consultants can be as risky as appointing a full-time fund-raiser directly to the staff, and almost invariably more expensive.

Consultants are adept at singing their own praises, so perhaps the main disadvantages of employing consultants should be summed up. Aspects of their work their literature never mentions are:

1. No consultant is going to feel particularly committed to

M

your cause. Generally, consultants will work for any cause, and this lack of commitment may make the existing staff of the charity unhappy about working with them.

2. Quite rightly, since they are only attached to your cause because of their fees, consultants will not do the actual asking for money, but see their job as telling the trustees how to ask. Thus consultants mobilize the charity's existing assets — and often after the campaign has succeeded the clients claim 'We could have done it ourselves', though in fact they needed the consultants to jog them into action.
3. The style of the consultants may not be appropriate to your particular charity. In recruiting staff, consultancy firms show a marked preference for retired military gentlemen and middle management from industry. They try to portray a conservative, 'professional' image, and as such as unlikely to work well with the staff of some of the newer, more radical charities.
4. Consultants are expensive. A charity has to pay not only for its campaign costs, and the costs of the firm's staff time (and generally this is much higher paid than equivalent staff directly employed by the charity), but on top of it all the charity has to pay a premium to cover the overheads of the fund-raising consultants, and also leave them some profit. (CORAT, which is a non-profit making group of management consultants which exists to serve charities, was in 1975 charging charities £50 a day for a consultant — and, let me repeat, this was on a non-profit making basis.)
5. Not all campaigns launched by consultants are successful. Of course, the consultants want to succeed, as they rely on recommendations for much of their new business. The reasons for failure may be ill-luck, poor judgment or bad timing; but whatever the outcome of the campaign the consultants take their fee. They do not suffer the consequences of their inefficiency: the charity does. Some examples are particularly disturbing — for example, the *Sunday Times* (23 May 1971) reported that an appeal to build an extension for Portsmouth Cathedral was being abandoned and, of the £72,000 raised, £45,000 was claimed in fees and appeal costs by the fund-raising consultants. Consultants refuse to work on a percentage basis — they claim it would be unethical and that no profession would be prepared to work like that. Those in

charities tend to disagree with this view, and think it unethical for the fund-raising consultants to take all the proceeds of an unsuccessful campaign.

6. Consultants who have been retained for a specific campaign may succeed in achieving their target, but alienate the charity's supporters, so that future fund-raising is made more difficult. Donors may find the consultants 'too pushy', resent the costs involved in the appeal, or dislike the style of the consultants' work, and may withdraw future support for these reasons.

How to choose a fund-raising consultant

Consultants are not vetted by any independent body, and there is nothing to stop any charlatan declaring himself a fund-raising consultant and opening a business. The National Council of Social Service will provide a list of consultants, but the best way to find a consultant is through recommendation, coupled with judicious vetting.

A charity can ask any firm of consultants to draw up a proposal for a fund-raising campaign, without being charged or feeling under any obligation. At this exploratory stage the proposals are not likely to be definitive, but they give the charity a chance to decide if they want to go ahead with the next stage of the selection process.

Some consultants confine themselves to certain causes, for example, churches or private schools, and may not be interested in your charity. Others restrict themselves to very specific types of appeal, for example, compiling charity brochures or organizing film premieres or finding industrial sponsors for sporting and cultural events. Others may think the chances of a successful campaign slight, and refuse the work on grounds of unsuitability. On occasion a consultant will suggest a feasibility study be carried out, to see if a campaign is likely to succeed. The charity would be charged for this, and should not authorize such a study until it has made a thorough investigation of the consultants.

Before asking for definite proposals and entering into any contract, the charity should ask:

1. For a list of past clients. Beware the list which has been pruned of failures. Ask previous clients if they were pleased with the consultants or disappointed, and for their comments on the firm in general.

2. About the firm's financial standing. Some investigation should be made into the consultancy's profitability, in case it goes into liquidation halfway through the campaign.

Specifically on the campaign the consultants propose for the charity, it should be asked:

(a) What they would do—will they set the target, devise the campaign, carry it through (or expect the charity to), prepare all literature and publicity, establish and administer a receipting and covenant procedure? How many of the activities are included in the basic fee?

(b) What do the consultants expect the charity to provide in the way of staff?

(c) What are they charging—and what does this exclude?

(d) Do they offer any safeguard against failure? For example, will they accept a reduction in their charges if the campaign is a failure?

(e) On what do the consultants base their estimated figures for money raised? How much of it is guesswork and how much is based on past experience of similar campaigns?

(f) How much of their staff time is included in their basic fee? Consultants will charge for any extra man-hours involved, so make sure that their estimate of time needed is sensible.

(g) That the charity retain the right to veto the consultants' choice of Campaign Director. He should have no obvious faults (like a drink problem) and should have experience of fund-raising. Ask how long he has been with the firm, and for details of his past campaigns. Make sure that he fits in with those working for the charity on a permanent basis.

Make sure that the consultants draw up a comprehensive campaign plan, and that it is agreed that it will deviate from it only after consultation and with the approval of the charity. The consultants will, in their proposals, usually give a time-scale in which the targets are to be reached. Look at them carefully to see if they are utterly unrealistic. Make clear to the consultants how involved you want to be in the day-to-day running of the campaign and the degree of information on the campaign that you expect.

Once you have found a consultant who can provide satisfactory answers to your queries, and produce a campaign proposal which seems attractive, then the time has come to think of signing a contract. It is prudent to include in any contract an unambiguous statement on what service is to be provided, for what fee, and to include a break clause with, say, two months' notice, in the event of either side's being dissatisfied. Incorporated into the contract should be all points on which the charity feels strongly—for example, the right to veto the choice of Campaign Director.

Many consultancies include in their campaign fee a continuation service. This should enable the charity to carry on with its fund-raising, to suit its future needs, and show it how to capitalize on the supposedly successful campaign which the consultants have just completed for the charity. Examine carefully the proposals of the consultants to see if this service is included, and ask past clients if the follow-up service was adequate.

Summary

Fund-raising consultants can provide an efficient service, and provide the charity with much needed funds. They charge highly for this service, but where they are successful few begrudge them their fees. Unfortunately not all consultants are competent.

Consultants are more likely to do too little than to involve the charity in risky schemes. They may try to cover up their lack of substantive progress by employing jargon, and attempting to mystify the whole fund-raising process; but an acid test can be applied to their work—either the money comes in or it does not.

In choosing a consultant, it is sensible to look for one who has successfully raised funds for a similar cause. The best guide as to the consultant's suitability is the opinion of his past clients, and time should be found to seek their opinion.

Fund-raisers appointed directly to the staff of the charity may be good or bad. The bad seem to outnumber the good, but this may reflect the incompetence of those making the appointments, not just the calibre of the applicants. A good fund-raiser is more committed than any consultant would be, and certainly less expensive. A charity's own fund-raiser is less likely to go for short-term success, and will be more concerned with building up the financial base of the charity.

Whether the charity decides to employ consultants or a fund-raiser directly to the staff, this does not relieve the trustees of their obligations to exploit their contacts and undertake a large part of the fund-raising.

Appendix North American fund-raising

Something of an aura of mystery has grown up in European minds about American fund-raising. *Per capita*, giving in the USA is thirteen times greater than in the UK and, even allowing for the difference in disposable income between the two countries, and the reduced need for charitable giving in this our welfare state, it does indicate an enormous fund-raising effort.

The tradition in this country of amateurism, and the increasingly outdated expectation that those working for charity should be unpaid, have retarded the growth of fund-raising consultants, who have evolved into a sophisticated professional group in the USA. Since the war, an increasing awareness of the success of fund-raisers in America, coupled with the establishment of fund-raising consultancies along American lines, has led to an interest and respect for American fund-raising techniques, without a very clear understanding of quite what they mean. This Appendix tries, through two examples, to show something of how different the fund-raising techniques are in North America, and to leave the reader to judge their appropriateness to the UK. Both examples are of Canadian charities, but the methods are typical of those used in the USA.

The Federated Appeal, Montreal

The Federated Appeal is what is referred to in America as a community chest. Local charities, and branches of national ones, apply for membership. They are vetted by the Federated Appeal, so that a donor may be satisfied that when giving to the Appeal he is contributing to well-run charities, and that his money will be spent in accordance with instructions laid down by the Federated Appeal. Participating charities thus lose some of their independence, and some charities will not join the appeal for this reason, preferring to run their own fund-raising campaigns. For small charities, without established support, membership of the Federated Appeal is particularly valuable. The Montreal Federated Appeal employs methods common to community chest appeals in the USA, but does not raise as much *per capita* as comparable USA appeals, because the tradition of charitable giving in this bicultural city is not yet established. The Federated Appeal of Montreal raises something in excess of £4 million *per annum*. This is how it is done:

The Appeal has a Board of Directors, of leading businessmen and other eminent citizens. They select a Campaign Chairman for the year—he is a leading businessman, the head of one of the largest corporations in the city. It is a great honour to be chosen, an honour which is conferred both on the individual and his company. The Chairman has the assistance of a permanent staff: they are his civil servants. As well as this permanent staff, the Campaign Chairman can call upon an advisory committee throughout the campaign.

The Chairman of the Campaign recruits the chairmen of the various committees from leading businessmen—again, it is a great honour to be asked. The overall campaign is divided into three main groups: business canvass, special canvass and communications and training. The last division deals with year-round publicity and, most important, the training of canvassers. Canvassers (that is those who do the actual asking) are the key figures in the appeal. Many young men aspiring to high managerial positions are keen to be involved in the Appeal, as it is an established way of securing recognition of competence. Firms will loan young executives full-time to the Federated Appeal, as a way of proving the company's service to the community, and also because it provides valuable training in sales techniques and management problems. Each volunteer is thoroughly trained in canvassing techniques.

The business canvass includes appeals to corporations both for company donations and to employees for 'payroll deductions'. The rule is that asking is done by peer group (or someone of slightly higher status). For example, the Campaign Chairman will ask heads of other leading corporations; a leading lawyer may ask other lawyers, who may be flattered by this token of his recognition. The Campaign Chairman and the volunteers lent to the Appeal by their firms assume the task of either asking for donations on a personal basis, or of asking people to do the asking for them. If the donor is wealthy and able to give generously, then great care will be taken in finding the right person to make the approach. The business canvass yields the greatest part of the Federated Appeal's revenue.

The special canvass division is responsible for appeals to professional groups, to trade unions and associations, schools and individuals. Appeals to schools and youth, in general, are much less developed than would be usual in a UK charity of comparable size. Nor does the Appeal attempt to establish local aid groups.

The Federated Appeal is primarily business-oriented. Apparently, the main argument used to persuade leading businessmen to contribute is that it is important to defend the private sector (i.e. charity) against the encroachment of the state. Firms expect to give to the Federated Appeal, even if they support many other causes or no others. The success of the Appeal depends on its being considered an honour to serve on one of its committees, which turns the onerous task of fund-raising into a pleasure rather than a chore. The giving is largely on a knock-for-knock basis: those asked will in turn expect a favour from the person asking—it is all genial blackmail.

Oxfam Québec—television pledging

Oxfam Québec is an independent charity, raising over £$\frac{1}{4}$ million a year. It achieves this amount with one full-time fund-raiser and a secretary. This truly amazing feat is achieved by using a method unknown to the UK—namely, television pledging.

Fund-raising is concentrated in a two-week campaign at the beginning of December. Of course, the planning and follow up go on throughout the year. The fund-raising is done with the co-operation of the mass media. Television and radio give free time, as do the poster display firms. In the campaign fortnight, the charity has a one-and-a-half-hour variety spectacular. The artists waive their fees. The television network is happy to be apparently philanthropic, by giving free broadcasting time, at the same time as saving money on producing a programme. On the show, the artists emphasize the need for funds for Oxfam Québec, and invite donations. This show launches the campaign. The television spectacular, with the stars giving their time, and phone-in pledging, is a popular technique for fund-raising in North America. It could not be used in the UK unless there were changes in the television charters.

Both local and national radio give free broadcasting time, amounting to fifteen to twenty hours. Some of this time will be used for phone-in pledging whilst the programme is on the air, donors can phone in and pledge their donations; some will be announced on the air; sometimes the announcer will just declare the total pledged since the beginning of the programme.

During the campaign fortnight, a random mailing to 150,000 people (whose names are selected from the telephone directory) is despatched. The response rate is 15 per cent, a success which can be attributed to the fact that it coincides with the blanket publicity of the fortnight.

All donations are received through the mail. There is no individual soliciting, and there are no special events—except those on the media, and a press conference. The charity does not expect to get donations from industry, which gives mainly to the Federated Appeal.

Oxfam Québec, like other Canadian charities, has short films for television commercials, and the equivalent for radio, as the commercial broadcasting companies do not always have sufficient paid advertising to fill the allotted time, so will slot in charity advertisements free of charge. These advertisements keep the charity's cause before the public.

Summary

Oxfam Québec and the Federated Appeal of Montreal use totally different methods of fund-raising, aimed at different donors. The Federated Appeal relies on the business community at large. Oxfam Québec reaches a mass audience through the mass media. The personnel of the Federated Appeal, whether voluntary or paid, project a business-like North American image: they would not seem incongruous in a board room, and use a great deal of American fund-raising jargon. Oxfam Québec as a whole have a much younger staff, Francophone, who would possibly feel uncomfortable in what they regard as the Anglophone business environment. Thus both organizations adopt the style appropriate to their type of appeal.

Index